Geared Up
WRITING Steampunk

Revised 3rd edition

BethDaniels

3 Media Press

GEARED UP WRITING STEAMPUNK

Dedicated to All
Fans of Steampunk!
Thanks for loving
this guide for years now!

Geared Up Writing Steampunk
© Beth Daniels 2014
Revision 2020
ISBN 9798693140356
Cover Design by Beth Daniels
Published by 3 Media Press, Bardstown, KY

All rights retained by author. Requests for limited excerpt rights can be acquired by contacting the author through the website, www.4TaleTellers.com.

The data, information, and suggestions made are those held by the author based on research and reading in numerous books labeled by publishers as Steampunk, Weird West, Gaslamp and other genre identification terms.

Various sections and chapters owe their creation to online workshops created and presented by the author although they do not appear verbatim as originally presented. All suggestions and evaluations are solely those of the author based on reading and writing in the Steampunk genre. This is the 3rd edition of GEARED UP: WRITING STEAMPUNK, which has slight revisions from the 2nd edition, released in 2014. The biggest change is in the addition of chapters on creating Steampunk machines, period jargon and naming characters and things, plus an expanded list of publishers. Four different sources were used to build the publishers list and then each was checked for information on their websites as well in March 2020.

The original volume was released in 2011 as WRITING STEAMPUNK. The contents changed more drastically between the 2011 and 2014 editions, but in any of the editions the focus has remained solely on writing Steampunk.

Introduction to the 3rd Edition!

In January 2013, IBM predicted that Steampunk was about to enter a new era. Major fashion retailers were posed to jump on the bandwagon. And why not? Over the past few years, the popularity of Steampunk has swelled – particularly when it comes to Facebook groups, online music and movie productions, and Steampunk specific conventions. All these folks tend to read Steampunk fiction, too. What prior to 2010 was a mere rill of Steam centered publications rose, swelling to proportions that would have Noah harvesting gopher wood for another go at an ark. This one would run on steam, of course, and likely resemble a dirigible more than an ocean-going vehicle.

Then it leveled off, though it was too tempting to lose power. Even urban fantasy bestselling author Jim Butcher entered the Steampunk lists with a new series.

Because so many tales have been released, either through traditional publishing houses, smaller presses, or via Indie publication, it was once again time to revamp the *Writing Steampunk* tome. Just as the 2014 edition kicked things around from the first one released in 2010/2011, the 2020 edition needed to reevaluate a few things, too. And add in new elements that were missing in the earlier editions.

This time out it isn't a total refitting of the machine, but definitely a tune up. The mechanics haven't changed, of course. The biggest change is the number of markets which swelled to 43! However, there is also a discussion on whether to use magic, paranormals, supernaturals, legendary beings (all normal for Gaslamp Fantasy) or not. Ones on The Empire's Lands, how to Create a Machine and Period Language. These weren't in either of the previous editions.

This isn't a book that guides you through the steps of writing a first novel. There are a lot of books and workshops and articles that can take you through that process. *Geared Up: Writing Steampunk* focuses on the elements that go into building a Steampunk world and scenario for a novel, novella or short fictional story.

So, without further ado, let's enter the parlour, saloon, or airship of your choice and prepare to enter the various worlds of Steampunk fiction!

Contents

What Is Steampunk
The Audience
The Stage
Magic, Shifters, Demons, and Such?
The Characters
The Adventure Tale
The Mystery Tale
The Romance Tale
The Dystopian Tale
The Comedic Tale
The Time Travel Tale
Shifters, Demons, and Such?
Magic Gears
Mangling History
World and Plot Building
Create A Being
Victoria's World
Edward's World
Weird West
Weird Urban West
Weird East
La Belle Épock
Other Worlds
Create a Machine
Period Jargon plus Naming People and Things
The Final Product
The Marketplace

What Is Steampunk

What exactly is "Steampunk"? There are several answers to this, depending on what the topic of conversation revolves around. It's a society of like-minded people, many of them interested in recycling. To others it is a spin-off of the Goth culture, though with brown dominating the color scheme.

There are Steampunk conventions specifically for those of a Steampunk mind and Steampunk pocket niches at various sci-fi/fantasy cons. There are bands, costumers, artists, and tinkerers redesigning modern technology to look like old technology. There are crafts people not only at the conventions but running online shops and Etsy businesses.

And there are writers living in Steampunk worlds of their own imagining and pounding out the mysterious, sometimes dystopian, sometimes comedic, and sometimes erotic, but nearly always adventurous tales set in pseudo Victorian worlds.

Steampunk fiction is a sub-genre of a sub-genre (alternative history) under the genre umbrella of Fantasy, and it has plenty of its own sub-genres as well.

The audience for Steampunk tales ranges from middle grade to young adult to the adult trade. And it covers the world. On Facebook alone, I belong to Steampunk groups in the US, the UK, Scandinavia, and know there are ones in Spain, Japan, Australia, and probably even places I just haven't seen a posting for somewhere. Steampunk is everywhere.

While Steampunk can encompass mystery, romance, and political statements, it is primarily an adventure format. There are exceptions, but we're talking about the 95% or better focus, and that's adventure.

Steampunk tales can take place anywhere on Earth, in a parallel dimension or universe, in the distant future or on another planet – the one requirement being that the society portrayed has quite a lot in common with the Victorian-Edwardian/Gilded Age/Belle Époch eras.

There are a couple things that excessive reading and deconstruction of published Steampunk fiction shows as required elements or at least highly recommended ones: building a pseudo Victorian-ish world and including at least one created being.

Before we can dive into either of those, there are a few decisions to make — actually, you've probably already made them but let's review the choices, hmm?

The Audience

The audience you have in mind will determine some directions on the route taken for world building. Pick one of the following:

Middle Grade (8 years old to 10 years old)
Young Adult (11 years old to 16 years old)
New Adult (16 years old to 25 years old)
Adult (18 years old and up)

Steampunk is a niche ridden subgenre and this gives you the opportunity to be domestic or exotic in the location you whisk your audience into. Therefore, the next choice is the place:

Britain
A particular British Colony
The Western US
The Eastern US
Canada
Australia or New Zealand
Africa
South America
Polynesia
The Near East
The Far East
India
Siam and adjoining countries
Tibet
Europe
The Arctic or Antarctic
A different dimension
A parallel universe
A distant planet

GEARED UP WRITING STEAMPUNK

Choose the time period (or the period to be modeled):

>Early Victorian (1834 to 1860)
>Mid-Victorian (1860 to 1880)
>Belle Époch/European (1871 to 1914)
>Old West (1870 to 1890)
>Gilded Age (1870 to 1890)
>Late Victorian (1880 to 1901)
>Edwardian (1901 to 1919)
>The far distant future
>The future within a generation or two
>The future within 100 to 300 years of C.E.
>Time travel back from the present
>Time travel to the future
>Time travel from the future

Note that the future doesn't always have to be reached via time travel, nor need a location in the past be reached via time travel.

There are stories noted as Steampunk that take place in earlier times, say the 18th century, but the Industrial Revolution was barely birthed in that period and it seems a stretch to include the 17th century simply because there will have to be *some* logic involved to explain the fantastic machines and other creations. This doesn't mean it can't be done, particularly if the events and discoveries are part of the backstory.

Now, will the story be foremost a/an:

>**Adventure**
>**Mystery**
>**Romance**
>**Literary***

*a story that doesn't involve adventure, mystery, or romance but rather centers around personal or emotional turmoil or discovery

Yes, your story can be a combination of all of these, but we'll work that out later. For now, knowing which is the primary "feel" of the story is important.

Next question! Is there a particular reason you choose the answers given for place, time period, or genre niche?

For instance, is there a historical event you'd like to use or remake? Do you already know a lot about a particular location? Do you tend to pick up a particular type of storyline to read for enjoyment and wish to stay within it though widen the boundaries with Steampunk?

All these elements figure in and it takes more pages to lay them out than it does to make the decision.

If you are writing a short story rather than a novella or a novel, some of the elements here might not be as important as others. Location may win out over time period, or the reverse, for instance.

Another choice to make, and it deals with the *tone* of the story. *Tone* refers to the "sound" of your text voice that readers hear as they read the text. Are they snickering, feeling depressed or fearful, getting aroused, or something else based on your writing style? It's all in the way you juggle your word choices and sentence structure. Therefore, are you aiming for:

Comedy
Dystopian
Erotic
Other

And one final piece of the basic puzzle deals with a choice of:

Urban setting (aka a city)
Rural setting (aka in the countryside or small town)
The Wilderness (desert, jungle, polar region, mountains)
Under the Oceans
Tunneling into terra firma
Venturing into the skies (or space travel)

In the event you are wondering why "another dimension" isn't in the list, well, chances are that that other dimension will have a landscape that looks very like one of those already mentioned.

All of these elements are ones that will catch a particular audience. They also help you build a very specific world or stage upon which your players will perform.

With choices made, let's move on to setting our stage!

The Stage

The 21st century audience is one that appreciates visual impact, and there is little doubt that Steampunk supplies quite a punch.

If brass goggles, corsets, bowlers, airships, and machines came to mind it is because these are featured in many tales, and on the covers of books and adorning the Steampunk enthusiasts as costume elements — well, perhaps not the airships, but wing insignia badges and pins would fill this niche's need. These items are the "face" of Steampunk, the accessories a reader is likely to expect. Does that mean they are a required element? No. The true *required* element is that *the society* your characters belong to is very like that of the Industrial 19th century or early 20th century. It just so happens that goggles, corsets, bowlers, airships and machines were extremely common sometime *during* the era.

Many storylines take place in Victorian London or a place that has quite a lot in common with Victorian London. But storylines can also be played out on a stage that is clearly the American West, the Australian Outback, the frozen poles, or the jungles of the Congo or Amazon rivers, or Mars.

And why is this? Let us adjust our microscope and take a look.

10X Magnification

These settings reflect what fascinated the people of the 19th century in particular, the things that created the look and attitudes of the 19th century. By the time Victoria took the throne in 1837, the Industrial Revolution was going full steam. Railroads had made an appearance and manufacturing was moving away from the old model of cottage-based craftsmen and craftswomen to the factory model. The Middle Class was growing in numbers, in influence, and in wealth. Higher education wetted the imaginations of science minded fellows as well as mechanics (engineers if formally trained) and sent them scurrying off to distant locales to study flora, fauna, and antiquities, to find cures for diseases and answers to questions that had either never been asked or had previously lacked the necessary means to achieve the answer. Adventuresome men and women went looking for the source of rivers, charged off to be the first to enter uncharted lands. Curiosity ran rampant in certain classes – the middle class and the upper class, for it took money to finance an expedition. If an adventurer didn't have the wherewithal personally, they needed connections to government coffers or friends and colleagues willing to toss checks their way.

The 19th century saw the real birth of geology and paleontology. Charles Darwin stunned, shocked and scandalized the Victorians with his ideas about evolution. Dr. Freud was inventing a new form of medicine, one that dealt with the psyche. Vaccines were being created. Photography came into being as did the telegraph, the telephone, and the electric light. Possibly, for the first time in history, invention in every aspect of life ran rampant.

And in this climate, the first science fiction tales were born. Invention was their mother, but they had more than one father for Jules Verne and H.G. Wells have an equal share of the credit on this particular birth certificate, but perhaps so does Mary Shelley.

They took what appeared in the newssheets, what made some people worried and others thrilled, and turned it to their own devices taking readers on journeys to the Moon, to obscure and mysterious islands, deep beneath the sea or toward the center of the Earth. Verne took his characters around the world in what was then an incredibly short length of time: 80 days. (After reading Verne's story, reporter Elizabeth Jane Cochran, aka Nellie Bly, did the trip in under 73 days, starting from New York in 1888, and traveling alone.) Wells journeyed through time in a machine, lured extraterrestrials to Earth, and made a man invisible. Mary Shelley, of course, built a man from spare parts with Victor Frankenstein's aid.

They weren't alone. Sherlock Holmes' creator, Arthur Conan Doyle, sent his Professor Challenger into *The Lost World* where extinct creatures still walked Terra Firma. Bram Stoker brought legend to life with *Dracula*. Oscar Wilde made a man fairly immortal in *Doran Gray*. H. Rider Haggard sent Allan Quartermain deep into unknown territory in a search for *King Solomon's Mines,* Robert Louis Stevenson supplied a fellow with a very split personality: *Dr. Jeckle and Mr. Hyde*. They were followed by Edgar Rice Burroughs taking readers to Mars with the adventures of John Carter and into the jungles of Africa with Tarzan.

Improbable adventures and yet not as improbable as they might once have been simply because technology and knowledge itself were taking seven league-like steps forward every day. While the pace was nothing like ours today, it was chugging along at a fantastic pace compared to only a decade or so before.

Therefore, our Steampunk stage, having grown out of the early science fiction tales of the 19th and early 20th century, reflects this.

What we tend to keep are elements of daily life: the wardrobes, the soot in the city, the dystopian life of the slums, the middle class gaining more clout than the peerage for the first time, the cozy but crowded and ornate décor, the Imperial colonies. Some tinkering is allowed but for the most part this is sacrosanct. Steampunk doesn't necessarily require "steam" but the society and structures that arose with the use of steam powered engines do tend to be a requirement.

The majority of Steampunk tales take place between the 1860s and the turn of the century. Yes, there are some that use earlier years and some that deal with World War I, but these are the fringe areas – usable but often not supplying what a particular writer has in mind for their Steampunk stage.

THE IMPROBABLY POSSIBLE

The style of storyline is truly diverse simply because Steampunk stories are ones of alternative history, even if they don't take place in a particular historical time. Our fathers (and mother) of science fiction were depicting their contemporary world but we are headed back in time (or borrowing elements of that time) and recreating it to fit our own fancies. Rather a reverse of what Verne, Wells and the others did in dreaming up what might be improbably possible in their world.

The Steampunk world is equally improbably possible, but it does have to have a certain logic behind it.

Not all alternative history tales are Steampunk, of course, but they do take an element (or more than a single element) and change it.

GEARED UP WRITING STEAMPUNK

From there these writers "what if" themselves a backstory that leads to this shift in historical fact and then let their muse run with it.

This leads to the first *rule* to follow when writing Steampunk.

HAVE A VERY GOOD REASON
WHY THE ELEMENTS IN THIS WORLD
ARE POSSIBLE

Some of the elements to take into consideration are:

- If a historical person who wasn't killed is now killed, what made this possible?

- If a historical person is saved or doesn't die as history prescribes, what made it possible?

- If a new technology (one that didn't exist in the time period) is introduced, what happened to accelerate the discovery or development of it?

- If a different side wins a battle, a war, what lead to the change or what made it possible?

In Mark Hodder's *The Strange Affair of Spring-Heeled Jack* the basic elements for the world the characters of his series inhabit is created. The subsequent books all take place in this world. What he has done is:

- Go into the still distant future where a suit that makes time travel possible is created. Our storyline doesn't stay there long for this has far more to do with backstory. Yes, backstory that doesn't happen in the past but in the future

- The creator of this suit travels back in time to stop an ancestor from doing something that has haunted the family. He plans to prevent his ancestor from committing the crime, and turns up in England in 1840

- In attempting to stop his ancestor, he inadvertently makes the crime worse and decides to zip back a few minutes earlier and try again so that what happened is prevented

- The second attempt ends with his ancestor being killed as well as the worse crime being committed. The trouble now is that if he doesn't do something quickly, without this specific ancestor he is going to cease to exist

- Inadvertently in attempting to fix things yet again, the traveler from the future creates the situations that grow into the odd legend of Spring-Heeled Jack. He is injured and the man who comes to his aid is a scientist

- Once the scientist gets his hands on the time travel suit all sorts of technology is developed that was impossible prior to this. It certainly didn't occur in historic fact

- Because of the crime that was made more heinous and the new technology, the 1860s world that Hodder's Captain Richard Burton (the explorer, not the actor) inhabits is a seemingly logical result

In the Steampunk American West world Mike Resnick created for his series, he simply altered things without much of an explanation by way of backstory, but what he does supply makes the situation logical. What he gives us is:

- A United States that stops at the Mississippi with the rest of the continent allotted to the various Indian tribes, although they allow temporary settlement and access to their lands for the purposes of mining

- He converts dime novelist Ned Buntline into a mechanical genius who works with Tom Edison, both having immigrated to Tombstone in Apache Territory to set up business, though they are covertly working for the U.S. government to figure out how to deactivate the magical control two particular shamen (one being Geronimo) have

- Then, in the first book, he gathers the Earps, the Clantons, Bat Masterson and Doc Holliday and arms them with upscale weapons from the shop of Buntline and Edison and maneuvers them near the OK Corral. Resnick sticks to history fairly closely in some areas for, although the world they inhabit has changed, the same people get killed, wounded, and assassinated as they were historically

Hodder and Resnick are brave fellows for nearly their entire cast is made up of historical personages. Most Steampunk tales don't take this sort of leap. Hopefully, that's good news to you.

Cherie Priest didn't use historic personages when she set up her Steampunk world, but she twisted various bits of history to suit her needs. Here's some of what she did:

- Stretch the American Civil War out so that after twenty years it is still going strong back East

- Move the Alaskan gold rush of 1898 so that it is in progress more than a decade earlier than it happened

- Had Texas decide it wanted to remain a republic and not be a state

- Destroyed Seattle turning it into a dystopian place for the few who live there

And because of the things she did change, the things she created were made relatively believable.

Scott Westerfeld took on World War I for his young adult Steampunk series. His changes included:

GEARED UP WRITING STEAMPUNK

- Charles Darwin coming up with the evolutionary theories but also discovering DNA

- The British going whole hog with DNA splicing and developing living creatures to take the place of many mechanical devices so that rather than dirigibles they have flying whales with crews living inside them, as well as other biologically engineered creatures

He did assassinate the correct historical personage to start the war even if the stage it now plays out on has altered.

Gail Carriger reconfigured things in London so that vampires and werewolves are considered normal in her Steampunk world.

George Mann has used a few historical personages, Queen Victoria in particular, but he has her living long past her 1901 death date thanks to machines that keep her alive.

These are merely a few examples but hopefully they give you a glimpse of what can and is being done in Steampunk fiction when altering history. We'll spend time doing this a bit later. In the meantime, let's return to our basic list.

Each of the Steampunk novelists I used as examples here were writing in the first fifteen years of the 21st century. I used them because 1) they supplied different styles of scenario, but also because 2) their work has been available long enough that I wouldn't be giving more recent series elements away. However, there is also a reason the late 20th century parents of Steampunk fiction are not mentioned. The reason for this is that the marketplace changes at a rapid rate. What was written in the 1980s and 1990s was miniscule compared to the Steampunk output in the 20-teens. That doesn't mean you can't get a handle on how to create a Steampunk world by reading K. W. Jeter (who coined the term Steampunk), Paul Di Filippo, Tim Powers, Michael Moorcock, Neal Stephenson, William Gibson and Bruce Sterling, China Miéville, James Blaylock or others. They were the forerunners of the flood that makes up the Steampunk library today. It was, after all, what they wrote that lead to what we write today.

What are these elements the fathers of Steampunk (you'll note the above list is dominated by men) supplied us with?

The Basic Steampunk Elements

When it comes to the elements that go beyond the early science fiction of the late Victorian and early Jazz Age, to the things that built Steampunk itself, we need a list culled from the variety of stories written in the past few decades.

- Victorian values or society in an altered setting which can be a twisting of historic events to similar places in parallel universes or dimensions, to other planets, to merely a future Earth setting (reference *The Diamond Age* by Neil Stephenson, 1995)

- Characters with magical abilities (reference *The Anubis Gates* by Tim Powers, 1997)

- Time travel (reference *The Anubis Gates*, Powers)

- Beings similar to those found in historically set horror or urban fantasy – in fact, think Victorian urban fantasy – like vampires and werewolves (reference "The Parasol Protectorate" books by Gail Carriger), zombies (Cherie Priest's books), angels, demons, wizards, witches, sorcerers, golems, homunculi, shape changers, body snatchers (in that they take over another person's body, reference *The Anubis Gates,* Powers), the Fae, gods from ancient and foreign pantheons, visitors from other worlds or planes or universes. At times, this runs close to Gaslamp Fantasy

- Technology arrived at sooner than historically possible (reference the card sorting machine – Babbage's Difference Engine actually built rather than simply designed – in *The Difference Engine* by Gibson and Sterling, 1990; *The Affinity Bridge* by George Mann, 2008; Westerfeld's *Leviathan*, 2009)

- Science related to biology that didn't really happen such as "Victoria" the giant newt that looks like Queen Victoria and is used as her double in Paul Di Filippo's *The Steampunk Trilogy* (1995) or the various mechanical limb replacements or cyborg-like creations that are both human and machine

- Exploration that never happened or didn't happen as portrayed (reference *Expedition to the Mountains of the Moon* by Mark Hodder, 2012)

There are many more references possible but those mentioned should give some idea of what has been done. If you are new to Steampunk, picking up the various anthologies of short stories will expose you to a host of settings and re-creations and alterations that illustrate extremely well what can be achieved in the worlds of Steampunk fiction.

More specific details will be worked out when we move to world building. But once the place and time and elements begin being juggled by your muse as it ponders the possibilities, it's time to put people on this stage. What has been worked out so far will indicate the type of characters they need to be.

The Characters

In most ways, the characters of Steampunk fiction are Victorians. Even those who are playing out the storylines in the Edwardian period are still Victorians because they were born (if they were real people) during her reign. There are several professions, avocations, backgrounds, social positions, etc., that they can feel at home in. What you choose to make them will reflect or direct the type of person they are and what they can be counted upon to do as the story plays out. Knowing that in a tale involving a quest the lead character is likely to be an explorer simplifies some of this process. If the place he is exploring requires him to understand a Himalayan dialect, that setting has also dictated an element of his background.

Let's look at the sort of "slots" a character can arise from based on classifications for the society in the 19th century.

The Inventor

Not surprising that this is the first possibility, is it? Invention gone wild is rather a Steampunk theme. There are clockwork movements and steam engines littering the minds of Steampunk writers – and probably in those of people who don't write but enjoy living in a vicarious Steampunk world. The Inventor is usually a mechanic, an engineer. They might be called upon to be a blacksmith to create what they design or merely have one on retainer. Inventors can be male or female (reference *The Girl Genius* graphic novels and the Agatha H. novels, both written by Phil and Kaja Foglio). Inventors can be heroes, secondary characters or evil masterminds – what they create and why they create it will likely determine their place in the cast. Put a spanner (wrench) in an inventor's hand or precise watchmaking tools and materials on his workbench and watch out! There are numerous historical models to use – both male and female (as the first dishwasher was invented by a woman).

The Diplomat

You can't escape politics – ever! You can change the results with a few tweaks though. In the 19th century Britain had the upper hand in a lot of things. England was the birthplace of the Industrial Revolution and thus had first dibs on new technology until much later in the century when a few Europeans and Americans began edging them out. It was technology that allowed the British Empire to latch on to territory around the globe first though. And once Victoria began marrying off her offspring and they began producing offspring of their own, nearly every royal house was related to Victoria (Europe's Grandmother) and Edward (Europe's Uncle). India was part of the Empire, prior to as well as during The Raj. Australia was British, the populace having grown with every prisoner transport that put into port. The Empire had a foot in Africa, contracts in China. The Czarina of Russia was Victoria's granddaughter. If the place wasn't under British control, there was likely to be a British connection and if not, then a diplomat was plopped down on the site. In real life Sir Richard Burton (explorer *and* diplomat) had one of these positions. And these positions weren't always in glittering places like Vienna, either.

With expansion, colonialism and Empire the catchwords – and not merely of the British – the role of a diplomat may well fit a character in your Steampunk world.

The Explorer

Why does one climb the once un-climbable mountain? Because it is there!

That wasn't always the reason explorers hied off into the unknown during the 19th century, so it shouldn't be their only reason in a Steampunk tale. There are all sorts of explorer types to consider. There are obviously the ones we'd term "Xtreme sports" types who do something to test themselves, or Fate, but the majority of explorers are looking for knowledge, for new things rather than an adrenalin rush. Historically there are numerous explorers to fuel the Steampunk author's imagination: botanists, entomologists (bug fanciers), biologists, archaeologists, geologists – the academically curious, in other words. Folks were journeying into jungles, up rivers, across deserts, through mountains, to the Arctic and to the Antarctic. They were headed so many different places and for so many different reasons, it probably seemed logical to readers when both Jules Verne and H.G. Wells sent characters to the Moon and Edgar Rice Burroughs dropped John Carter on Mars.

In Steampunk there are stories of penal colonies on Mars rather than Australia and plans to send garbage to the moon to act as compost over the years to make it habitable. For the most part, there are plenty of places on Earth (or that it's possible to get to on some connected plane or dimension, or wherever places like Shangri-La are) for exploration, particularly if a character can't sleep for needing to know the source of the Nile or the Amazon or where-the-heck the Northwest Passage might be.

Explorers are also adventurers like H. Rider Haggard's Allan Quartermain, Doyle's Professor Challenger, or an Indiana Jones type.

The Explorer-Diplomat

Strange category, huh? But many diplomats were also explorers and many explorers were diplomats. I've already mentioned Sir Richard Burton but there were others who weren't quite as well known. In fact, some of the best ones to harvest from historical fact were educated lady explorers who had to be unofficial diplomats considering they ended up meeting people who kept their women folk under their thumb in many cases. Otherwise, the job of diplomat in some places meant there was plenty of time to kick one's heels and exploration of wherever they'd been posted offered a humdinger of an outlet for the frustrated ambassador or consul.

The Scientist

Where the inventor tinkers with mechanics, the scientist plays with biology and chemistry and other naturally occurring phenomena like electricity. Several discoveries were made in the 19th century, from Darwin's theory on the evolution of species to aspirin. As aspirin isn't very exciting (though after a particularly trying day in the lab or in the field a Steampunk character might need to dissolve a paper of Bayer aspirin in water anytime from 1898 onwards – wasn't available in pill form for a long time), there are plenty of opportunities here. Over-the-counter poppy based drugs were legal in this time period (in fact Coca Cola used cocaine in the recipe, though that ingredient was replaced long, long ago), and think what could happen if a substance like LSD was created to augment them?

It's difficult to decide whether to term Thomas Edison and Nikola Tesla as scientists or inventors as they worked with mechanical devices – awesome ones, but still mechanical. Fellows like this straddle both the categories (let's call them **The Scientist-Inventors**) as they did wondrous things personally, and Edison's Menlo Park teams brought a new way of developing inventions into being.

For our Steampunk purposes though, the lone scientist working on projects is the more likely candidate for modeling a character on. There are more than enough of them around in the historical archives to inspire you – again, both male and female.

The Industrialist

This fellow is the creation of the Industrial Age. He owns factories, mines, railroads. He's gone beyond being a merchant to being a man with power. His institutions create the new serf class, the workers who toil in terrible conditions for minimal or sub-minimal wages for long hours and range from children to women to men. Depending on the decade involved, these can be textile businesses (weaving cloth) to factories where clothing is made, or something else is mass produced, like matches. While there will be laws created to limit some of the dystopian situations the workers live in (length of hours, age limitations to prevent the extremely young from being employed both in factories and mines), this is probably only an irritation to him.

He's of the middle class and his wealth is coveted by the peers whose net worth in Funds has dropped considerably. He might be British; he might be American. In either case he has daughters he's willing to barter to get a title in the house.

Of course, not all the industrialists are cruel, money grubbing types. Some build housing for employees with company stores (though money isn't exchanged here usually, but vouchers or coupons are, and that keeps them chained to the company). Some are involved with charitable organizations.

The Merchant

The merchant has been around for quite a while, his position blossoming in sync with the towns during the medieval period. His ancestors may have been plying the same trade for decades, centuries. These aren't the traveling tinkers but businessmen and women with shops. Their place in society might have begun with the guilds but has expanded. They may or may not actually make the merchandise sold in the shop. Imports will fill shelves as well as locally made goods.

Hatters, cobblers, tailors, seamstresses, book sellers, book publishers, green grocers, tavern owners, hotel owners, wagon and carriage makers, horse dealers, saddle and other leather goods makers, butchers, bakers, candlestick makers (though the better homes and businesses are lit with gas light for most of the Victorian with electric lighting arriving by the close of the century), carpenters, masons, master chimney sweeps... Well, you get the idea, right? People who sell goods or offer a specific service.

The Royals

With the period named after the royals (other than in the United States or on the Continent), they obviously can and have appeared as characters in Steampunk fiction.

Victoria, obviously, is the figurehead of the British Empire and can be considered a retiring individual or a force to be reckoned with. She never forgave her oldest son, Edward Albert aka Bertie, aka Edward VI, for Prince Albert's (her husband, his father) death. Not that Bertie caused it other than in Victoria's mind — Albert had hied off in a huff to berate Bertie when the heir to the throne took up with a woman of dubious virtue and by the time Albert made it back to the palace he was ill and subsequently died of the illness. Victoria could hold a grudge a long time and refused to allow Bertie to be involved in concerns of the government although he'd one day be the King. He was given reports but that was all until the 1890s when she bent enough to involve him in some things (probably after a lot of pleading by her advisors to consider the future).

With no duties to perform, Bertie became a playboy. He was very social and traveled quite a bit, making friends easily. While he was married, he never stopped enjoying a variety of ladies, having mistresses who were peeresses, commoners, entertainers. In 1901 when Victoria died, he assumed the mantle of king though he held it for only a short time, dying himself in 1910. The remaining nine years of the Edwardian Era have George V on the throne and in 1917 he changes the family name to Windsor to distance them from their German relatives.

Besides Victoria and Edward there are a host of other royals that could be incorporated into a Steampunk tale. Victoria and Albert had quite a few children, who married and had quite a few children.

It's worth noting that Prince Albert, the Queen's consort, was extremely interested in the inventions being turned out not only by British subjects, but in other countries around the world. He was the force behind the Great Exhibition in the 1850s. Depending on the era chosen for your Steampunk tale and the tweaking done to historical record, Albert could figure as a character, even if a minor one.

Or the future George V could.

The Reformers and Missionaries

Mostly we're talking Church of England here, though other Protestant sects can apply. The rising middle class were church going sorts and charity organizations were formed quite regularly. Orphans homes and homes for unwed mothers appeared. In 1852 William Booth began taking his Christian message to the slums, converting those termed "godless" – they were definitely destitute, suffering, and stuck in areas of rampant crime. His ministry grew to include ten full time workers and then grew even larger. It wasn't until 1878 that the "Hallelujah Army" became the Salvation Army though.

Clara Barton formed the American Red Cross in 1881 but she'd gotten the idea from the Swiss when she visited Europe after the American Civil War and learned about newly organized groups dedicated to the care and rehabilitation of soldiers maimed in the various wars.

Clara is an example of the involvement of women of the Middle Class in the charity movement. Women were frequently more likely to visit the homes of the poor than their male counterparts in the various organizations were, but that doesn't mean that there weren't men who did so as well when not at the office. And there were numerous organizations which means creating your own is equally viable.

Particularly if you are going the dystopian route with your Steampunk fiction, the inclusion of a charity worker to the neighborhood is worth considering.

The Socialites

No matter how depressing the life of a large chunk of the population is there are those at the top of the ladder who are ready to dance the night away. The Victorian/Edwardian era, the Gilded Age (in the U.S.) and the Belle Époch (in Europe, particularly France) provide settings where if you had money or status, there was a place to flaunt it. Conspicuous consumption, the historians call it.

Socialites did it in spades. But then they had time on their hands, particularly the younger set who grew up in the lap of wealth and were in expectation of inheriting it. When in the city there were clubs, balls, and an assortment of other activities. Matchmaking involved money and connections. Mrs. Astor decided there were only 400 families worth allowing in her door in New York City. When the city became unbearable it was off to the countryside to "cottages" that look suspiciously like mansions or to family estates. Visiting by friends within the closed circle (for the circle was closed no matter what the country) was encouraged.

The young men did go into the family business (unless they were peers, then it was the Army or government). The sweet young things did marry within the circle. While the men collected degrees from Oxford, Cambridge, Harvard, Yale, and similar places, a few of their sisters attended college as well though more often they were sent off to finishing schools where they could make connections with other girls in the right circles. Switzerland had some nice schools. Otherwise it was frequently governesses for the girls and tutors, perhaps a public school for the boys (Eton and Rugby are but two examples), which were the male equivalent of a finishing school and preparation for university, law, the ministry or the Army – no matter where the young man in question was headed, it was at public schools (or private schools outside of the British Empire) where connections with other families of power were made.

There was a very active marriage market for young women whose fathers' had made vast fortunes in business, both American heiresses and those of British capitalists. The wealthy middle class were fishing for peerages for their daughters and the peers were trawling for fortunes for their sons. Winston Churchill's mother was one of the American heiresses to land a lord as a husband.

While there really is no age limit on the type of character who is a socialite, for the most part picture these as the younger generation (girls in their late teens and very early twenties; young men in their twenties) who are being groomed and maneuvered into alliances by their elders who serve as the hosts of various entertainments.

Doesn't mean they can't lead the young astray or use them. Socialites can hold down various positions in your cast of characters, including victim.

The Servants

There are servants and there are servants, right?

For instance, if you watch *Downton Abbey* you're familiar with the hierarchy: butler, housekeeper, valet, personal maid or dresser, cook or even on occasion a chef, footmen, upstairs maids, downstairs maids, kitchen help, and then there's the groundskeeper and his staff, the grooms in the stable, the carriage driver or chauffeur once automobiles come into fashion. There's the estate manager, the master's secretary (male, of course), the mistress's companion or nurse if required, a librarian (male again) should the master be bookish or a lab assistant should he be interested in the sciences. Depending on the ages of the children there are tutors and/or governesses (both of whom aren't really servants but aren't family either), nurses and nursemaids. In some households there might even be personal parsons or at least a minister who owes his tenure at the local church to the master of the house.

It takes nearly a personal village to keep the country estate running.

What if some of these positions are allotted to created beings though or augmented with machines more familiar to the 20th and 21st century household?

The Spiritualists

It doesn't matter whether you're on the east or west side of the "pond" (the Atlantic Ocean), for spiritualists were busy running séances to get messages from those in the great beyond and manifesting ectoplasm for spirit visits in Britain, on the Continent, and in the U.S. As Steampunk is most often concerned with the British or the Americans, there are a myriad of historical sources to access and alter as you please.

Most of those whose names made it into the historic records were hoaxes, of course, con men and women who preyed on those desperate for contact with their dearly departed. Harry Houdini made it one of his goals in life to debunk many of them. He even wrote books (still available!) about how these people accomplished the things that seemed to prove they were the real thing.

Of course, this element works well for Steampunk whether the visitations are real or not!

Members of the Royal Society

The Royal Society of London for Improving Natural Knowledge is a good place for Steampunk characters to hang out. They don't actually need to be an explorer to belong, but if they are an explorer looking for financial backing for an expedition, this is the place to go. Until they changed the membership rules, that is. Then it was scientists only (1847). That shouldn't bother us though as scientists are characters, too.

The Military

The officers, infantry, cavalry, able bodied seamen – lots of fellows looking good in their uniforms...or rather scruffy in them should they have been on the march long.

And lots of places they can be engaged in war, too! There's unrest in India – the Mutiny of 1857 – and territorial struggles in Africa (Zulu War, the Boer War) for the boys in the red coats. They have a bit of trouble in the Crimean, too (Charge of the Light Brigade comes to mind). The Boxer Rebellion concerns China as do the Opium Wars.

In Europe there are revolutionaries, border disputes, all of which seem to culminate in World War I, the war to end all wars, except it didn't.

In the United States if we follow the Gilded Age, we have the various Indian wars, and beyond those the Spanish-American War, the contretemps with Poncho Viva on the Mexican border.

And the Steampunk period actually shares time with Dieselpunk (diesel powered engines rather than steam powered ones) for the Great War (aka World War One), 1914-1918.

The military is always interested in what inventors can dream up in the way of better weapons – maybe even for invincible soldiers and seamen.

The Spies

Nothing gets done without the aid of spies and the British Politicals were very involved in The Great Game with Russia. These fellows were frequently officers who managed to train themselves to blend in and pass for locals. Deep undercover stuff.

They were active in India, the Near East, and anywhere else their governments wanted inside tips on what was going on. Naturally, if caught, things didn't go well for them.

For our purposes it might be more industrial spies than political ones in the arena. Could be a combination, too!

After the American Civil War, the "Secret Service" was formed but it wasn't involved in protecting the President until much later – it was more concerned with illegal tender, but that can work well for Steampunk, too.

Organizations like MI5 and MI6 and their North American and European counterparts don't really come into being historically until the Edwardian era. Since we're altering history, you can tinker with their beginnings, too. One of the most famous spies of the WW I period is Mata Hari, of course.

The Urchins

Street children in the city, in other words. Horatio Alger made a career writing about boys who made their own way on the streets and managed to find lives off the street (*Ragged Dick* is an example...from shoeshine boy in New York City to something better). Sherlock Holmes used these children as his Baker Street Irregulars. Dickens' *Oliver Twist* is one.

What they offer in the way of possible characters are their criminal associations. They are pickpockets, shoplifters, purse thieves, frequently trained by a Fagan type and working either as teams or alone. They hold horses for a copper (a coin, not a police officer), can be used to carry messages, might be attempting to care for younger siblings or ill parents and working at legal jobs (newsboy, in a factory, as a chimney sweep if small and thin) and supplementing wages with thievery. They could also be professional thieves and proud of their prowess in their chosen field.

There are urchins fending for themselves or for their families in London, Manchester, Edinburgh, Glasgow, New York City, Chicago, Philadelphia, Paris, Rome, Constantinople, Cairo – basically any large or major 19th century metropolis. Their lives are dystopian for the most part as they live in the worst conditions and are preyed on by stronger forces. Particularly if you have middle grade or young adult Steampunk stories in mind, urchins are a very good resource for characters. They work well at running errands or gathering information for your good guys or being used horrifically by the bad guys. Pip Ballantine and Tee Morris have a group of them who do surveillance for Miss Braun of their Ministry of Peculiar Occurrences Steampunk series.

The Thieves and Pirates

Naturally *thieves* are grown up urchins in many cases, though they can also come from the middle or upper class. Adam Worth was a master thief on both sides of the Atlantic and was involved in safe cracking, con games, illegal gambling, jewelry theft, and whisking paintings done by old masters from their frames. A character modeled after *this* Worth (as in the same period another Worth, Charles, ran an exclusive dress design boutique in Paris) could make an escape in an airship piloted by pirates.

Airship pirates turn up in quite a lot of Steampunk, actually. Frequently they, like their ocean-going counterparts many decades before in the Golden Age of Piracy, have stolen the ships and either ship contraband or raid other airships. If you are considering a Steampunk set in a space traveling future, the set up with the Firefly class ship *Serenity* of the TV show *Firefly* and subsequent movie spin-off *Serenity* give an updated version of pirates in aircraft. Cherie Priest also has airship pirates in her dystopian Steampunk world.

The Resurrectionists

Sadly, this is a classification of possible Steampunk character that those engaged in building their own beings or constructs that are part biological and part mechanical will fancy doing business with. Resurrectionists first went into business when medical men (and artists like Da Vinci) wanted to know more about the human body but were not allowed to actually obtain bodies of the dead to study unless the deceased was a common murderer turned over to them for dissection (part of the punishment, no doubt) or because the Church (Church of Rome as well as the Protestant ones), and thus the government, made the practice illegal.

If you were a scientist with an interest in building your own brand of Dr. Frankenstein's monster, then you needed to do business with the body snatchers who raided the graveyards shortly after a funeral. Wait too long and the "product" wasn't in decent enough shape for the "consumer" to use it. Guards used to be hired to watch over the newly buried for a specific number of days to ensure that departed loved ones weren't retrieved by Resurrectionists. Doesn't mean the guards didn't look the other way, though, if paid to do so.

Excellent addition to your character possibilities if building beings from spare parts is in your Steampunk scenario.

The Entertainers

There have always been entertainers, of course, even around early mankind's campfires. What the 19th century offers us is the rise of the music hall and of actors, actresses (they wouldn't have liked being called *actors*), vocalists, musicians and speakers (many of them authors) making the rounds on both sides of the Atlantic.

While the circus has its beginnings in the 18th century in London, it is during the 19th century that it leaves the "home" arena and begins traveling, frequently via train, to towns...particularly in America. The Wild West Show (like Buffalo Bill Cody's) was also a "road" show.

It didn't always take singing, dancing, aerobatics, lectures or comedy routines (burlesque and vaudeville are doing well in this era, too) to merit the label of "entertainer" though. P.T. Barnum had a museum of oddities long before he became involved with the circus, though he should be credited with the addition of the midway sideshows as a circus attraction. Among those in this category we can add nature's unfortunates, the "freaks" that people paid to gawk at: Siamese twins, hermaphrodites, the "elephant" man, dwarfs like Tiny Tim, those born missing limbs or with extra limbs, etc. Some became quite famous. Frequently being "on display" was the only employment they could find as they were often ostracized otherwise by society.

Because entertainers of various types move around a lot, they can be used in Steampunk as spies, minions, and other imaginative cast members. Several sideshow-like elements work their way into Steampunk. Enough, in fact, to merit it a niche in Carniepunk.

The Socialists and Anarchists

Here's where history intrudes but also offers benefits. Karl Marx ended up living in London, chased off the continent, although his ideas lingered. There were several rebellions as the downtrodden workers rose up against the long-established aristocratic regimes throughout Europe. What happened in Russia during the Edwardian period is the best remembered of these, of course, probably because it resulted in the deaths of the Romanov ruling family – Czar Nicholas, Czarina Alexandria and their children – and the rise of Stalin's Russia.

Although many socialist uprisings weren't on that scale, there were governmental changes in various places. Steampunk villains are no doubt on the lookout for ways to manipulate these to their own designs.

The real danger to Londoners frequently came from the Fenians, In 1851 there were 110,000 Irish-born people living in London (by 1901 it was down to 60,000) and Irish independence was an issue that frequently turned violent. The Clerkenwell Outrage of 1867 is an example where to free a jailed countryman due to hang, a 60-foot-wide hole was blown in the wall of Clerkenwell Prison. It was the people in the surrounding homes that suffered with 12 killed, 40 injured and, it was claimed, 20 infants "died in the womb" as a result. This was just one of the terrorist atrocities linked to the Fenians. To deal with them Scotland Yard created a special department, the Special Irish Branch, which later dropped the "Irish" from their name. They were plain clothes detectives as well as undercover cops.

Whether it is socialists or Fenians causing a ruckus, your Steampunk characters could get involved and alter circumstances – for the good or for the bad.

The Immigrants

Immigrants figure prominently in the 19th century because as the factories rise, the populace leaves the bucolic limitations of rural communities to seek jobs. They also arrive various places having fled conditions in their homelands or because they were shipped to a penal colony or sent to watch over things in a penal colony.

We tend to think of immigrants as foreigners, and they are that, even when they move from one section of a country to another. In the 19th century there were very few people who left the place where they were born. Heck, their ancestors hadn't done so, so why should they? Jobs – that's the answer. Because progress brought things like vaccines and better living conditions (okay, maybe not in the slums, but overall) there was a population boom in the 19th century.

In any case we have an influx of people from rural areas, many of them women, looking for jobs in the factories.

We also have people escaping political turmoil in Russia and various German states. The Irish are in London (in particular) for three reasons: the potato famine, to wage that terrorist war for Irish freedom, and to find employment.

The Irish stream to America as well, but the mines in the Western territories, like California, Nevada, Colorado, etc., draw people from China, Australia, Peru, Mexico, and Europe, thus immigrants of various nationalities (as well as those hailing from various necks of the Eastern states) can appear in your Steampunk Weird West world.

In New York City the Irish are very visible as the Tammany Hall political machine fills the police force with the newly arrived as well as 1st and 2nd generation Irish Americans. The largest and most powerful criminal gang is the Dead Rabbits, an Irish gang. In fact, prior to the turn of the century, nearly every major gang in power in the grimmest parts of New York was Irish in makeup. Around the turn of the century Italians join these gangs and by the 1920s the Irish have pretty well been replaced by them.

The population funneled into Australia and its nearby islands (Tasmania, New Zealand) was the result of London courts emptying the prisons by transporting able bodied men and women (and convicted children) to their shores. A few officials, troops to keep them in line, and people looking for homesteading opportunities showed up as well. Pip Ballantine and Tee Morris's Steampunk comedy-mystery-adventure series uses not only Pip's native soil (New Zealand) as their heroine's home, but integrates the way people from the colonies were looked down on by certain elements of society in London.

Considering that Steampunk tales can also take place in other dimensions or on distant worlds or supply time travelers, characters who could be considered immigrants are everywhere!

The Writers

Literacy was on the rise. This gave birth to the "yellow novels", what we might call penny dreadfuls or dime novels, and to investigative journalism.

Nelly Bly was the penname of the most famous of these journalists, possibly for the fact that she was female as well as willing to go undercover to get to the heart of her subject. She wrote an expose on conditions for female factory workers and spent ten days undercover in an insane asylum for another assignment. As mentioned earlier, she even decided to test whether Jules Verne's Phineas Fogg could have made it around the world within 80 days. She beat that, going around the world, from departure in New York to return in New York, in 72 days, 6 hours, 11 minutes, and 14 seconds. And did it mostly without a chaperone, a nearly unthinkable way for a young unmarried woman to travel in the era.

Louisa May Alcott, Mark Twain, Henry James, Charles Dickens, Oscar Wilde, Arthur Conan Doyle, Robert Louis Stevenson, and of course H.G. Wells and Jules Verne are extremely famous and popular writers. Alcott is probably the only one of these who didn't do a lecture circuit (though her father attempted one). But the writers work that a lot of 19th century readers would inhale were dime novelists like Ned Buntline in mid-century and Col. Prentiss Ingraham from 1869 until his death (200 handwritten mostly 75,000 word long stories later) in 1905. Pen names abounded and Louisa May Alcott used a few when she wrote for the story press papers as well.

Although the stories were fictional, a lot of the people reading them (or having them read to them by children now required to attend school) believed everything was real. In some case the people were (Calamity Jane, Wild Bill Hickok, Jesse and Frank James, Buffalo Bill Cody, etc.) but most of them were not. Writers who spun tales set in the American West frequently packed up their typewriter in later years (as typewriters hadn't made it to very affordable or portable dimensions until the close of the century) and hopped on a train, pounding out their stories while ferreting out locations and personalities to recreate in more noble ways. Melodrama ruled in the yellow press tales.

When it comes to characters who are writers you have a choice of dime novelist, investigative reporter or famous scribbler. Any of them would work well in Steampunk.

The Crushers

If you haven't read many stories set in the 19th century urban world, whether alternative history or using a historical setting, you might not know that "crushers" are the police, particularly in London, but any New York City gang immigrant might call them by this term, too. Coppers is also used, possibly more often in America than in Britain.

The 19th century is when the modern police department came into being. It started with Robert Peel in London and the formation of the Metropolitan Police to replace and upgrade the previous system (which had included the Bow Street Runners. . . bounty hunters, really, as that's how they got paid) and men of the Watch. The Peelers (The Metropolitan Police) in London were soon referred to by another name though, one based on the address of the main headquarters' public entrance which was located at Number 7 Scotland Yard, though the building's official address, or front entrance, was at Number 4 Whitehall. Constables were added in greater numbers and special divisions came into being when required. In 1883 the Special Irish Branch (mentioned a bit earlier) was created to deal with the Fenian terrorists. In 1890 "Scotland Yard" moved to a larger headquarters on the Embankment but had resigned itself to being "Scotland Yard" to the public by then. The move would figure into things should you set a story after 1890. Yes, Steampunk is alternative history, which means you could move the location or never have them leave Whitehall, but the quarters would be cramped if they stayed.

Peel's Metropolitan Police worked so well that the model was picked up and copied in the 1850s by New York City, Boston, and other urban centers.

In Paris Eugène Vidocq, a thief turned thief catcher, was instrumental in the birth of the Sûreté, in 1812. Originally staffed entirely with former crooks who worked undercover, the Sûreté was very successful. Scotland Yard sent men to Paris to observe and talk to Vidocq about how his team worked. Unfortunately, the uniformed French police thought the disreputable Sûreté men were scandalous. They shut Vidocq's organization down and rebuilt the Sûreté with one new rule – no former crooks need apply.

Between the Sûreté and Scotland Yard, the police forces of today have their foundations. Forensics would follow beginning in the later Victorian with mug shots and fingerprinting among the innovations.

The police can always use a hand from inventors when it comes to weapons, protective gear, and even assault troops. There were no S.W.A.T. teams historically, but that doesn't mean you need to avoid having one. Maybe even staff it with robots or mechanically enhanced officers.

Investigators

Private ones rather than official police or government types, that is. You can think Sherlock Holmes or you can go with real life organizations like Pinkerton's National Detective Agency.

GEARED UP WRITING STEAMPUNK

Allan Pinkerton, a Scottish immigrant to the U.S., was a cooper (barrel maker) who then joined the Chicago police force but in the 1850s he opened his own investigative agency based on the success he'd had in solving crimes while a member of the police. He hired a variety of people to work with him, an upholsterer, a salesman, and in 1856, a woman, Kate Warne, who had convinced him that women were frequently overlooked where a man would appear suspicious. By the late 1850s, there were fifteen operatives employed by the Pinkerton National Detective Agency. He preferred the term *operatives* over "detective" but apparently felt the public would understand what they did better if "detective" was used. By 1884 when Allan died, leaving his sons William and Robert in charge, there were 2,000 full time employees and a couple thousand "reservists" to be called up when needed. Pinkertons' company motto was "we never sleep", so perhaps they had security elements of a Steampunk sort on the night shifts.

England also had a few private detectives by mid-century, though rather than "detective agencies" they ran "private inquiry offices". Charles Frederick Field was one of these. He came off a stellar career in crime solving as a Yard man, though he'd only joined the newly established force in 1829 because he needed a job. He started as a sergeant with E Division, moved on to L Division and became an inspector with the Woolwich Dockyards section. From there it was on to the Detective Branch in 1846 where he ultimately sat at the Chief's desk. Having once aspired to be an actor, Field frequently made use of disguises. Retiring on December 2, 1852, he opened his own Private Inquiry Bureau which kept him actively involved in chasing criminals until 1865 when he retired from private inquiry work as well. Dickens likely used him as a model for some characters and was instrumental in getting Field's name in the press, so you might consider using him, too.

One of Field's employees at the inquiry office, Ignatius Paul Pollaky, aka "Paddington" Pollaky, left to open his own office, Pollaky's Private Inquiry Office in 1862. His successes led to popularity in the 1870s and being the model for a character in an 1881 Gilbert and Sullivan show. He retired from investigative work in 1882 and had a reputation as a chess player in Brighton. Pollaky is one of our immigrants though, hailing from Hungary, and didn't become a British citizen until 1914. He had applied for it in 1862 and been refused – in fact, government records listed that original application under "applicants of doubtful character" and called him an adventurer.

Pinkerton's wasn't the only detective agency State side for David J. Cook, a former militia major general from Colorado opened the Rocky Mountain Detective Association and concentrated on sending his employees after bank robbers, cattle rustlers and occasionally murderers.

W. H. Triplit opened the Ohio Secret Service agency in 1883. The Sherman Detective Agency was in business in 1917. Though he's out of our time period, some altering of history could benefit from looking into Harold K. "Hal" Lipset's ability to "bug" nearly anything – including a martini olive.

In France, if you recall, the Paris police shut down Eugène Vidocq's style of Sûreté, but that didn't stop Vidocq who opened his own private inquiry office after getting his walking papers. He continued to hire only former criminals, use disguises, work stings, and continued to maintain the wide range of informers he'd built as a policeman. He built his business into one with a reputation for getting the job done promptly.

So there are historic models to use and detectives, whether private or otherwise, are definitely a classification for a Steampunk character. Fortunately for some of us, both Allan Pinkerton and David Cook wrote books about the exploits of their operatives. Vidocq wrote about his own exploits, in French, naturally, though there are translations and numerous books about him, too.

Lawyers and Barristers

Depends on which side of the pond you're on for these – counselors answer to differ things and could well have different sorts of jobs. While a barrister does the courtroom thing, a legal counsel/solicitor in Britain doesn't but probably does wills and act as a go between when a barrister is needed. We're not only dealing with different sides of the Atlantic and different countries, we're dealing with different eras, too, and that could make a difference.

Another difference between the barristers of Britain and the lawyers/attorneys of the United States could be in the training. In the U.S. this wasn't acquired by attending college so much as it was in working with someone who already was a lawyer, thus one learned this trade by being a legal eagle's go-fer and research assistant – perhaps it would be akin to a modern paralegal being trained by their boss to be admitted to the bar – and not merely the one down the street with boot rails, spittoons, and barrels of beer and whiskey. In any case, many men in the legal trade were trained by their mentor/employers in the 19th century. The more rural the setting, the less likely previous schooling of a higher level is likely to be a requirement.

In Steampunk we are writing alternative history fiction, but this is one of those professions where nearly everything would need to stay rather historically accurate. That's not to say some tweaking can't be done, but my suggestion is to keep any tinkering minor. You can always create *new* laws for your characters to deal with. Can't you see a barrister or lawyer with a mechanical "search engine" law clerk though. What the solicitor or attorney deals within your tale will depend on whether you need them to have a specialized field, like criminal law or patent law.

The White Slaves

White slaves aren't necessarily people sold into slavery after being captured off a ship, though if your story involves the Barbary or Ottoman pirates of the Mediterranean, it's a viable element. In the early 1800s Napoleon's navy, British sea power and even the infant United States' navy were involved in tromping the pirates' power. They were non-existent once the French colonized North Africa in 1830, though for our purposes they might simply have moved elsewhere and grabbed a dirigible to use a few decades down the line.

These captives are only one type of white slave though because the conditions in which people worked in the factories were also considered something that turned them into white slaves. There certainly was no way out of such a life other than death or maiming by a machine – something that lost a person their job and made them destitute.

The sex trade was another white slavery niche, one that had been going on in the cities if innocent girls had been arriving from the country in search of employment. Kindly featured madams or even couples would meet the stage coaches (and later the trains), fix on girls who looked both fearful and excited to be in the city, and offered to help them find a place to stay and employment. Once inside the bordello the only way out was to lose their looks, contract a disease (if that bothered the clientele), or die. There was next to no chance to obtain a respectable position once a girl was forced into the mattress trade.

Boys were also abducted for similar uses. Despite having a reputation as an extremely buttoned-up society, the Victorians had very active vice riddled opportunities available every evening.

For Steampunk purposes, tales have been written featuring totally mechanical sex dolls and humans enhanced with whatever the writer has dreamed up, turning them into cyborgs of pleasure.

Likewise, those maimed employees at the factory could also be turned into cyborgs of the factory line.

The Illusionists

Because there were so many stages looking for performers, "magicians" were frequent additions to the bill at theatres around the world.

There was no magic involved in these acts, of course. It was all slight-of-hand and misdirection, mechanics (to make things disappear and appear) and chemistry (those puffs of smoke to "disappear" or "appear" within).

Looking into the lives and performances of Victorian stage magicians like Maskelyne, Carl Hermann, John Henry Anderson, Giovanni Bartolomeo Bosco, Ben Ali Bey (who was actually from Bavaria), David Devant, Robert Heller, and the two men who inspired Edwardian illusionist Harry Houdini, Robert-Houdin and Harry Kellar. These men's lives should supply a plethora of ideas. It certainly did for the folks responsible for the storyline in *The Prestige*, didn't it? Heck, they threw Tesla into the mix!

The Aviators

Of course, we think aviators with Steampunk – all those airships! And because these are "ships" they will need crews, thus cast members from tinkerers to galley cooks to maintenance staff to captain and any other officer class needed – depends on the size of the ship and the sort of ship it is.

George Mann has had airships manned by mechanical men, so that's possible, too, although best to read a lot of Steampunk involving airships to ensure that your set up is individual.

The 19th century had numerous balloons in the air and the fellows flying them will be aviators of a sort, too. Phineas Fogg (Verne's character in *Around the World in 80 Days*) engaged one for part of his trip, didn't he? Balloon corps were used in the various wars to get an eagle-eye's view of what the enemy was up to and where. Naturally this made the assignment dangerous as if you could see them, they could see you and there had been rockets used by the military since Wellington was in the Peninsula in the Napoleonic Wars early in the century. If the exploding envelope of gas didn't kill you, the fall out of the sky certainly would.

Lots of folks in Britain, on the Continent and in the U.S. were working to go beyond balloons and beyond the manned winged glider to create aircraft that used an engine and could still be air born when manned. There were a lot of near things and a lot of disasters until the Wright Brothers (Wilber and Orville) of the U.S. accomplished the first such vehicle. After their 1903 success they went home to their bicycle shop in Ohio and improved their flyer, filed a patient and waited for it to be granted. The moment it was (around 1908) Wilber loaded the plane on board a ship and headed for Europe. When he came home in 1909 it was with enough contracts for planes to make a bicycle shop redundant for the family. Bi planes are really big during WW I, as we know from tales of aviators like Baron von Richthofen, the Red Baron. Wing-walking and aerobatics (aerial stunts) are big hits during the "barnstorming" years (1920s), but they could be done earlier for another reason.

This illustrates that your aviators can be inventors, mechanics, or pilots. Having more than two aboard a fixed wing flying machine prior to 1920 was either rare or uncommon — which certainly opens the options on what you could do with planes. Of course, if you improve them, you'll need to put the upgrade in World War I and that might change the outcome, depending on which side has that upgrade. Chances are both sides would have them once the technology was available — spies if not similar ideas in the creators' minds supplying them.

Don't forget that aviatrix heroines who crash in yet unexplored jungles could then have amazing adventures, accompanied by cobbled together R2D2-like companions made from the parts of their plane. Eminently doable in the Edwardian years. Aviators could do the same, too.

While Graf Ferdinand von Zeppelin was tinkering with ideas for his creation (the Zeppelin) as early as 1873, the large airship doesn't really make headlines until the Edwardian years. The design isn't consolidated until 1893 and was patented in Germany in 1895 (1899 is the date of the U.S. patent filed). Commercial flights on zeppelins (which became the common name for all rigid airships) began in 1910. Nearly everyone in Steampunk has put these monstrous airships into action earlier than history — or the *graf* — did.

The first helicopter really belongs to the Edwardian era, however, Leonardo Da Vinci did draw an "aerial screw" back in the 1480s. A look at his idea might inspire your mechanically inclined aviation enthusiast character to create something different than we're used to seeing. Gustave de Ponton d'Amécourt, a French inventor, not only coined the term "helicopter" in 1861, he tossed together the first steam-powered model. Although it used a new building product — aluminum — it still didn't get off the ground.

In 1885 Thomas Edison put his mind to building a helicopter but as it kept exploding and injuring employees, it was left to another team of brothers, the Breguets in France, to get the first "gyroplane" to lift off in 1907. Still, it wasn't really until the 1920s that inventors began getting all the necessary components working in sync to create a helicopter that was reliable enough for anyone to want to purchase one. As you know by now, that doesn't mean you can't have your own team of Steampunk inventors overcoming the problems all of these fellows faced.

The Paranormals, the Fae and Spirit World Characters

What a leap! Flying machines to otherworldly beings. Otherworldly in that they aren't human or never were, that is.

These break down into different categories – more specific ones.

Paranormals are beings that were once human and are not human or only partly human or passing as human now. Frequently they got this way because they were bitten: vampires and werewolves. Perhaps zombies, perhaps not. Depends on your creation story for them. As ghosts were once human, they slot in here.

Beings of spirit are not paranormals because they weren't "normal" to begin with in many ways. Beings of spirit are angels, demons, djinn, devils, gods and goddesses, and beings that might have gods for parents but are monsters (three headed dogs, Cyclops, minotaurs, etc.).

The Fae are otherworldly and come in many types: fairies, brownies, gremlins, dwarfs, pixies, elves, etc. There are also the animals of the fae: unicorns, dragons, griffins, etc.

Other things that can fall under this heading are things created or animated with magic: mummies, golems, homunculi, and sometimes zombies (as they are part of the Voodoo world).

None of these are required in Steampunk but they frequently show up in it. Put this down to the blending of urban fantasy and historical period, though you may have or hear of a different view. Anything is possible.

Gail Carriger created a heroine who is not human, nor is she any of the already mentioned beings. Therefore, dreaming up something different is also possible if they are a natural being, not one built specifically by one of the other Steampunk characters.

Heroes of the Classics

In some cases, these are characters who are related to the gang in the category above – but these are people who have *one* parent who isn't human. Hercules falls in this category because his father is Zeus, but his mother is human, however, he isn't a god himself. Could also be those given a gift by a god, like Sampson's strength is related to his need to avoid barbers.

Considering Arthur Pendragon is supposed to return when Britain needs him, he could fit into this slot. Odysseus could, and so could Helen of Troy because their stories have been around for a really, really, really long time. But not as long as that of Gilgamesh, whose epic life is recounted in the oldest know written book in the world.

Whether it is via someone traveling back in time to snatch them up and return them to the Steampunk period or that your creation story has made them immortal, they and others like them could show up in your altered world. Heck, if something happened to Queen Victoria or the Union and the Confederacy wanted a well thought of judge to decide their issues, a time traveler could pluck Solomon from his court and put him to work in the 19th century. Think of the culture shock he'd experience! Unless, among the wonders of his court he had something like the Antikythera mechanism that really interested him.

The Created Beings

This is the category that is *the second law* of Steampunk: **there must be created beings.**

These created beings don't have to belong to the villain of the piece, they are merely beings that did not exist in the 19th century. They can be humans who have lost limbs or bodily functions and have had these "parts" substituted with mechanical or biological replacements. In the 19th century a carved leg or hand or hook would replace a lost limb. The loss of anything else that kept a human alive was fatal – there were no substitute parts. At least *historically* there weren't. This is Steampunk and thus clockwork or highly unlikely and inappropriate biological parts could be grafted to the person (or animal – build a faster racehorse?) in question. The result of this augmentation is a created being – they could be good, bad, or merely running a shop one of your characters visits.

Created beings don't have to hold down jobs as major characters, although they could. A created being can be sentient or not. It could merely be a clockwork or steam powered creation.

It's much easier to see created beings as mechanical creations, automatons, robots. It could be a cyborg, that half-man, half-machine that frequently ends up being a minion. Doesn't have to be a minion though. It all depends on you.

A created being can be the product of a lab as Di Filippo's "Victoria" is, a newt grown large enough to resemble a woman of short stature. It could also be the result of an experiment gone wrong.

Even Dorian Gray could be considered a created being as the man walking around certainly isn't the real Dorian Gray totally, which is the man in the portrait, though he probably ends up in a category of his own – one related to magical manipulation.

Naturally werewolves and vampires fall under the created being category as their new persona is not the same as their original one. Same goes for zombies and mummies, golems, homunculi, and anything resembling Victor Frankenstein's monster – whether it has the monster's personality or not (from the book, not the movies necessarily). And yes, we did put them into the Paranormal group, but they belong in both categories. Crossbreeding?

So to recap here, a created being is any character or element that is ambulatory, reached its current status or appearance or capability through the aid of a doctor, technician, mechanic/inventor or mad man (reference here is *The Anubis Gates*). It can be sentient but can merely be a machine, too. It can be a creation of magic or of a bite from a similar being.

Remember, when it comes to Steampunk, probably 98% of all fiction written includes a created being of some sort. Frequently more than one. All it takes is reading widely in this sub-genre to spot all types of created beings.

Alternative historical tales set in the Victorian era that do not have created beings or machines tend to fit the Gaslamp Fantasy category rather than the Steampunk one.

Now that we have setting, year, tone, and characters, let's move on to the type of plot line that can be spun.

The Adventure Tale

Adventure rules Steampunk.

Well, it does in most fantasy, doesn't it? Steampunk is part of the fantasy pantheon of sub-genres and wouldn't fit nearly as well without a quest, a search, dangerous situations, breathless anticipation and in many cases, a "save the world" – or at least a particular part of it – scenario.

The eras earmarked for Steampunk harvesting are riddled with historical events that lend themselves to the adventure tale.

We have explorations, wars, the expansion of the Empire or the thrust of Imperialism made by other European countries and the United States.

We have wondrous inventions – real ones! – to act like a seven-course meal for our muses.

There are incredible discoveries made from the bones of dinosaurs to the ruins of the Mayan empire in South America and, if we "steal" from the early 1920s, the richly appointed tomb of King Tut and the accompanying "curse of the mummy" to spark imaginations. An adventure tale can include a mystery and/or a romance as well. It could involve time travel, dystopian situations or be a comedic tale, though I'm treating each of these as a category of their own.

The decisions here are:

- Searches for lost things. These can be things lost back in history such as the exact site of Sodom and Gomorrah, Solomon's palace or various misplaced mines (the Lost Dutchman Mine, for example). Lost ships, obviously carrying treasure of some sort, and treasure isn't always precious metals and gems. The Library of Alexandria had a nasty fire but was everything there lost? The Holy Grail and other historic religious artifacts are supposedly lost. People can be lost even if they don't realize they have been misplaced – Dr. Livingstone simply thought he'd been out of touch while

Stanley and others considered him lost. Lost tombs of kings. Lost continents such as Atlantis and Mu. The Anasazi and other tribes that appear to have gone mysteriously missing. What about ships in or out of the Bermuda Triangle?

- Searches for legendary items. The Holy Grail could land here, but so can Excalibur, Camelot, the Round Table. The Philosopher's Stone to create gold from metal or the "recipe" for immortality. The Seven Cities of Cibola, the Fountain of Youth. A crystal skull. The impenetrable armor of Achilles, a flying carpet, Noah's Ark, The Ark of the Covenant, the Helm of Darkness (makes wearer invisible), Apollo's Bow (causes health, famine or death), plus various flying machines or things that allow the owner to be a shape shifter. And this is just a sampling of the list of things that comes up online in a search for legendary artifacts.

- Searches for legendary places such as Shangri-La, El Dorado, or any place that gods were said to reside or that the dead were sent (Purgatory, Hell, Tartarus, across the River Styx). The Northwest Passage. Heck, until it was discovered by a single-minded amateur, even the city of Troy fits this category.

- Searches for legendary creatures such as dragons, unicorns, the abdominal snowman, Big Foot, the fae, or even undiscovered tribes.

- Searches for scientific reasons (flora and fauna collection, excavations at tels and in the Valley of the Kings, excavations for dinosaur bones with the dawn of paleontology), expeditions into jungles to uncover the secrets of ancient civilizations, such as the Mayans or Olmecs (stumbled across in the 19th century). We can also include exploration beneath the sea, to the interior of the Earth, and any successful shots at the Moon or Mars your characters might choose to make. Making contact with indigenous peoples can also fit here.

- Searches for geographic answers. Finding the headwaters of the Nile and the Amazon were hot 19th century topics. Visits to the poles were ones in very different climatological conditions. Climbs to the tops of the Himalayas and other peaks were favored.

- Searches for lost knowledge, which can be in nearly any direction you wish to take it, be it magically based, related to technology (such as the Antikythera mechanism), even simply strange and still unexplained things like the Nazca lines or the properties of ley lines, what places like Stonehenge really were, the key to making Greek fire or something worse.

- It can be about stealing something or someone, too. It can be about getting even, exacting revenge.

The action-adventure doesn't have to leave London or whatever other urban setting you might be using because explorers and scientists were always lugging things home with them. If you want to include a mummy's curse, there is nothing stopping you.

The key to the adventure part of the tale can be in the quest itself. You can look to Rider Haggard's *King Solomon's Mines* or any Indiana Jones movie or take a page from elements of fantasy tales for a visual (or mental) picture of setting your characters forth if they are on a fact finding mission or determined to make a name for themselves. Not to mention take home a bit of treasure if it offers itself.

An adventure tale doesn't have to be a quest though. It can also be a race to protect something or save something or rescue it (or a person) or escape from something in society or from someone. It can be to beat someone to something. With all the Empire building being done in the 19th century, and into the early 20th, having villains who want to control things, or take over, or be in power is a logical scenario. When you add in the strictures placed on women (many who had begun demonstrating to change the system), and the surprising number of women who took off exploring on their own (usually because they were not only strong minded but they could afford to do so), changing the world was already a goal for many.

An adventure tale doesn't have to be "high" adventure though, it can be low key as well. A tale where aid is given to save someone living in the slums or to escape a brutal family life can be just as much of an adventure as tromping through the jungles and coming face-to-face with a far from extinct T-Rex is. The difference will not only be in the terrain, but the adversary. Danger will exist in both situations.

An example of how a Steampunk adventure tale might play out is:

The Scientist/Adventurer/Quest scenario

Scientist develops a way to travel to the planet Mars and announces at a Royal Society meeting in 1876 that he, his wife and his daughter will depart the next day for the Red Planet, their destination the Forests of Mars.

There is an uproar.

There is no evidence of forests on Mars. His answer is that if he were on Mars and turned his telescope toward Earth there would be no way to tell whether there were forests on Earth either, ergo, he will either prove that there are forests on Mars or prove conclusively that there are not.

Absolutely insane to take women along he is told. His answer is that it was their own decision. His wife could not bear to be parted from him and his daughter has long been his assistant in all scientific exploration he has done, even though until this time it has been restricted to the laboratory and observatory. She is an intelligent and strong-minded young woman (a suffragette) and has threatened to stow aboard if not included in the expedition.

With this as the start, here are various ways the story can go.

- They do not return when expected and another adventurer sallies forth to find them (a la Stanley in search of Livingstone). He might have a ship that does time jumps as his invention is the time travel vehicle

- They might reach Mars with no problem, sail along in the atmosphere checking oxygen levels and looking for evidence of forests and stumble upon an unexpected civilization underground, or creatures quite unlike (or very like) those that do inhabit Earth or did inhabit Earth (again, underground as we know Mars is a desert but one with evidence of water in the past). Their ship could be damaged either way, but small, swift robotic messenger vehicles are launched toward Earth to acquaint colleagues of their discovery and plight, and request a second expedition be sent

- Instead of a stalwart time traveler, the second expedition might be made up of men determined to harvest the mineral wealth of Mars for their own industrial purposes (and to stock a museum with creatures from the Red Planet), or for their own advancement in scientific circles and thus the members of the first expedition must be gotten rid of

- Or the original scientist could suffer a personality change (or have hidden his true nature) and set about destroying the members of the second expedition, or his rescue party, or the civilization he finds on Mars

- If the time travel machine was involved in the original expedition, they might catapult far enough back to when Mars wasn't as desolate, either on purpose or by accident

- To wrap the story up there could be a rescue party arrive from Earth (one that hasn't already been worked into the story), there could be no rescue party and the members of the expedition are stranded to live out their lives on Mars, in which case if there is a second and younger scientist worked in, he and the daughter could be the Adam and Eve of a new civilization on Mars...although this would mean that their children will need to mate to provide a third generation and that might put them off...or they could simply expect that by that time there will be more arrivals from Earth, too.

In other words, from the first premise of the story there were several paths to take and some of them could be combined or edited to fit together. The scenario has space travel of two varieties that still haven't been reached today, a romance, a plot by single minded investors or fellow scientists, the possibility of unknown civilizations being discovered as well as territory claimed for the Empire, and possibly a rescue but possibly not a rescue but still a fairly happy ending.

An adventure-tale will need to have 50% or more – in fact, this is a case where *more* is better – close escapes from something. As it will all take place in a Steampunk world, the type of world you build will have a lot to do with the adventure encountered.

Let's move on to see how writing a Steampunk mystery scenario can work.

The Mystery Tale

While an adventure doesn't require a mystery, frequently a mystery is part of an adventure. The decision on whether to focus more on the mystery to be solved or the adventure to be survived, is naturally up to you.

A Steampunk mystery can feature characters who are with Scotland Yard, are private investigators (such as consulting detective Sherlock Holmes), be government men and women, scientists, academics, scholars, officers, physicians, reporters, or even thieves.

The standard set up for these types of mysteries work well for Steampunk, but there are other mystery styles to consider as well.

A cozy is generally set in a small rural town that is generally sleepy until something astonishing occurs, such as a murder. For the Steampunk spin it might involve a reclusive intellectual or the daughter of the local watchmaker who has done some tinkering of her own, or a retired battlefield veteran. The set up for a cozy mystery is retained but the world in which it happens has been altered to Steampunk specifications for both the stage and how a murder (or other crime) occurred. Certainly, a victim found with an animatron's iron gauntlet crushing their windpipe would lend itself to suspecting the nearest scientist-mechanic.

A police procedural, of course, will involve Scotland Yard's various divisions. There are several stories using the Special Branch, but they aren't the only available detectives to call in. When things out of the ordinary occur, or an occult angle appears to have been the cause, government investigators might be brought in. This happens in both Pip Ballantine and Tee Morris's Ministry of Peculiar Occurrences series and in George Mann's Newberry and Hobbs Steampunk mysteries, and others.

The amateur detective could be defined as a Sherlock Holmes type character who isn't in business as an investigator, but if it was really Dr. Watson who solved the crimes, he would also fit this category. Think of the main character as someone untrained as a police detective but working in a metropolitan area. The key with the amateur detective style mystery is to have the crime occur within the main character's forte (as in using a doctor's knowledge of medicine or an inventor's knowledge of mechanics, or the spy techniques used by a former soldier who worked in intelligence gathering being the element that gives them a leg up in the investigation required). The crime might be limited to their neighborhood or niche in society so that they are looking for information among people they know well or know someone who knows the suspects fairly well. The amateur detective always needs to have a police officer in their camp to make the official arrest, so put one in a "cozy" style story, too.

A Steampunk mystery could also be a caper, that is, involve a thief who is implicated in a crime they didn't do and needs to prove themselves innocent of or who is involved in planning a heist. For Steampunk purposes, they would naturally be using uncommonly updated technology to aid in the theft, though as good usually triumphs over crime in mysteries, something will have to fall through so that what they went after isn't necessarily what they end up with.

What with the Great Game in play with British and Russian spies jockeying for information along the Afghan borders and in India and China in the 19th century, and other nations attempting to grab what 3rd world territory England hadn't snapped up yet, espionage tales suit Steampunk well. Add in industrial espionage and the deal is done, isn't it? Just think what the 19th century version of Q could come up with in toys for a mutton-chop wearing Bond to use.

The reverse mystery is another option. Here the reader has been in on the crime, knows who committed it, how it was done, and why it was done. The "reverse" is that the story is the detective figuring it all out and keeping the reader enthralled as they do so. Tricky huh? A very un-Steampunk example of a reverse mystery is the old *Columbo* television series.

The suspense tale can be any of these types of mystery, but it can also be a serial killer type tale. The 19th century offers quite a number of these fellows (and a few women doing people in, too), with Jack the Ripper in London and H. H. Holmes in the Chicago area heading the list. Some say they were the same man as the Ripper's crimes predate Holmes' by a year or so. The Ripper was never identified, though many names were put forth (and still are being put forth), but

Holmes was caught and executed following his unrepentant confession. He didn't, by the way, mention anything about ever having been in London. In a Steampunk tale such murders could be committed by a Mr. Hyde type (the product of a scientist's work) or by a created being inefficiently harvesting organs for an evil creator, too.

The serial killer angle has proven to work well with romantic suspense where the budding romance between targeted victim and protector takes up half the plot. No reason one of them can't be a tinkerer or scientist. Take Dr. Frankenstein out of the Regency period and plunk him down in the cholera pandemic in London in the 1850s and have his monster (scavenged from the victims of the epidemic) come after him for revenge. In Mary Shelley's book, the monster was out to get even with Victor, after all. Perhaps a comely police matron could be assigned to keep a protective eye on the doctor – or she could be a government agent as the Yard didn't actually *have* policewomen yet. They were a 20th century addition. The matrons had jobs dealing with the women prisoners brought in. Still, where there is a will, there is a way to write a romantic-suspense style Steampunk mystery.

Now, for an example scenario for a mystery set in a Steampunk world, let's try this spin on our original adventure idea.

Our scientist has been able to obtain funding and the nod for his trip to Mars from the government because they are interested in snagging further territory for the Empire, territory that isn't within the reach of other governments. Or so they believe.

Unbeknownst to them, the man who has been courting the scientist's daughter is in the employ of Thomas Edison who is frustrated that his Menlo Park lab is turning out inventions tied to the domestic world: light bulbs, phonographs, movies, etc. He craves to make those who deride his creations as toys eat their words. He has had a Mars project on his secret drawing board for years but has been frustrated by the propulsion system needed to escape Earth's atmosphere and ensure that the trip isn't of an unendurable length. Thus, he has hired a spy to steal the technology he needs to move ahead on the prospective trip.

Because the spy originally was only playing at courting the scientist's daughter after landing a job as the scientist's assistant based on a false resume (though he does have a knack for building things himself), he is torn over whether to be loyal to Edison, the man who sent him, or to the man who hired him without checking his credentials, or to the girl he has since fallen in love with – who is quite a hand in the scientific world herself. When the scientist is discovered in his lab with the metallic hand of a robot buried in his chest, the spy...

- Fears that his credentials will be checked, and his covert assignment discovered

- Fears that Edison has gotten tired of waiting and sent a mechanical assassin to do away with the scientist based on the spy's last report which claimed the man kept his discoveries hidden in the lab and never left it, both eating and sleeping there, thus preventing their theft

- Fears that someone other than Edison has also been after the scientific discoveries

- Fears that the girl he loves is now in danger because she intends to go ahead with her father's voyage of exploration to Mars

Thus, our spy is about to become the detective, but also will be protecting the woman he hopes will still have him once she knows why he had wiggled into her and her father's hearts.

We might never make it to Mars in the mystery version, but we had the wherewithal to make the trip possible.

A mystery will need to be 50% or more about the crime committed and the search for the perpetrator as well as the arrest or death of that perpetrator, the fact that it all happens in a Steampunk world means that the crime will probably need to make use of available Steampunk weaponry or machines, or even a created being, to keep eluding capture.

Although there was a touch of romance in the mystery scenario, let's see what we could do with a Steampunk tale sans adventure or mystery but with fond sighs and perhaps a few exchanged kisses scattered through it now.

The Romance Tale

In the old vernacular of the 19th century, a tale of romance was merely an adventure tale. In the 20th and 21st century, though, such is not the case. It's a relationship story between two lovers. They may not start out as that but by the end of the story their fate to remain together for a happily ever after is usually sealed.

There are various sorts of romances, of course, so let's take a stroll through the rose covered bower and consider how love stories can be a part of a Steampunk world. The trick is to remember that a romance is a relationship story so the emphasis is more on overcoming interior and exterior difficulties the two main characters have that keeps them apart until the conclusion of the story when it looks like a happily ever after is within reach. That said, let's look at the types of romance storylines and how they might be refitted for Steampunk.

One type of romance is the historical romance, which the Steampunk romance will be unless it is set in the distant future, and even then, it will incorporate 19th century values and *morés* to lend itself to Steampunk. As a historical romance though there is the option to not alter quite as much of the world with alternative history traipsings as happens in the adventure tales. The story will still require things such as created beings or awesome machines. One or both major romantic characters might even have enhancement of a mechanical type. Perhaps the scientist/mechanic doing the fitting of a replacement limb or the nurse caring for the patient and keeping the new limb oiled will be part of the couple headed for romance. Or you might create an early version of a physical therapist who helps the newly enhanced party to learn to work with the new attachment and in the process becomes the love interest.

It is possible to write contemporary romance (that is, a story that takes place in the 21st century) that has Steampunk elements but it will be only partially set in the contemporary world – Steampunk tales are alternative history so some warping of history will be necessary. The way to keep it more "contemporary" is to have the romantic couple *both* be from the "real" world (21st century) and in some way travel either back in time or to a parallel universe or dimension. If they were strangers who got sucked into the Steampunk world of your creation, then their story is one that focuses on not only falling in love but in building a life in this new world...unless they are figuring out a way to get back "home", that is.

There is also the option to go the route already paved by historical romances that feature time travel. In these sorts of tales a character from the contemporary world has usually travelled back in time, which would suit our purposes very well. They could also have, as our example couple might have done, landed in the parallel universe or dimension. A character from the Steampunk world could also travel forward in time but there will be at least two things to include in this scenario: 1) the Steampunk machine or created being will need to come with them and 2) unless they are arriving from a different universe or dimension, the fact that they are from the story's past will mean there will be changes in the contemporary world that are related to that Steampunk world.

So, while not entirely un-doable, a contemporary romance that incorporates Steampunk elements can be tricky. A contemporary romance that revolves around a couple meeting at and living in a community that embraces Steampunk elements while the rest of the world remains as it is – you know, like the world we're living in – is merely a contemporary romance, not a Steampunk genre tale of romance.

Contemporary romances are frequently romantic-comedy stories and putting this type of spin on a Steampunk set storyline is also possible. Romantic comedies are, after all, stories in which manners or customs or culture clashes entangle a pair of witty, klutzy, or cornered characters. Imagine *You've Got Mail* using in-the-home telegraph connections to send messages that are then posted in the personal sections in the daily newspapers, and the covert communications turn out to be between rival animatronic competitors. Obviously, the time traveler from the contemporary world could be one of them.

Take away the contemporary element and keep the comedy and chances are you will find stories similar to Gail Carriger's Parasol Protectorate series.

But what Carriger's work leads us into is also the Steampunk paranormal romance. In this type of tale one of the romantic couples, or both, is a vampire or a werewolf, a witch, a sorcerer, a demon, or angel. Head back to the list of paranormal, legendary, or spirit character types for ideas here. The elements included or excluded in this Victorian set paranormal romance will determine whether the story is a true Steampunk story or is a Gaslamp style. No fantastic machines or created being making an appearance? Then you have a Gaslamp fantasy romance. Bram Stoker's *Dracula* is probably a model for Gaslamp romantic suspense. The same could be said of Oscar Wilde's *Dorian Gray*, though it's not a romance, it is more Gaslamp in style.

Back in the Mystery section romantic-suspense was mentioned. There are various types of romantic suspense though: the type where the romance is the main feature and the type where the romance comes in second, though the race is close. The trick then is to come up with a guideline. For something where the romance is of paramount concern, let's say more than half of the story will center on and have scenes peopled only by the romantic couple. For romantic suspense where the mystery is the winner, the romance section might take up a third of the storyline, maybe a bit more but never be half of it. Considering the Steampunk elements still need to be worked in, the best idea might be to have them linked to the suspense part of the story rather than the romance section.

One way to handle the division might be to have an ongoing relationship in a series so that the evolution of characters from being partners to being something more is how it all comes together. The reader can see that the lead characters are attracted to each other but not acting on things yet in the first book, but they will move closer to a romantic relationship as the series stretches out. An example of how this can be done is Pip Ballantine and Tee Morris' take on it with Miss Braun and Mr. Book's building relationship in the Ministry of Peculiar Occurrences books.

The Gothic romance is a type of romantic suspense for it has the heroine putting herself in danger in a mysterious mansion where she has gone to be either a companion or nurse or governess to a woman or child. The setting is frequently a landscape where Mother Nature can be just as threatening, such as the moors of Devon or Yorkshire, the cliffs of Cornwall or similar situation. And in a gothic the master of the house appears to be sinister and capable of dark deeds, perhaps even suspected of them, yet the heroine will be drawn to him and he to her. She will fear the worst of him until the very end of the story when he rescues her or is involved in rescuing her (they may have become trapped together by the true villain, after all).

The Gothic lends itself to the dystopian side of Steampunk with its atmosphere but at heart it is a romantic-suspense tale. Still, what better for a Steampunk set up than a master who retreats to his dungeon workshop where no one can enter but his assistant, but from which strange sounds are heard? While there isn't a romance other than as an element of Victor Frankenstein's life that the monster wishes to destroy (and the woman in question dies), the gloominess of *Frankenstein* (the book, which is quite different from the movies) with Victor's creation of the monster is an excellent model for a Steampunk tale. We do, after all, have a created being in *Frankenstein*.

The Erotic romance will have a number of bedroom scenes (even if they don't always occur in the bedroom), and can include elements that the Marquis de Sade would give a thumbs up to, though on second thought, he might find them tame, too. Let's say they are so far into the R rating that X could well apply. I'm not sure whether there is a storyline or not as the few people I've met who read erotica never mention a plot. For Steampunk purposes we don't necessarily need a plot (though one should be essayed if at all possible) but we do need that created being that is totally mechanical, partly mechanical, or was never a biological that Mother Nature had on her drawing board of evolutionary adjustments to any species. These stories can also be ones where the romantic partners aren't limited to just two. Threesomes also apply. Maybe a male, a female and that created being? Specific programming might be necessary, if so.

Perhaps what the erotic Steampunk romance needs most is a way to titillate within a Steampunk world. There are sections in Gordon Dahlquist's *The Glass Books of the Dream Eaters* that do this. If an erotic romance set in a Steampunk world is your goal, the best option is to read what is available in the marketplace. The majority of these titles tend to be available as e-books, so they are easily acquired.

Another type of romance is the same sex relationship. As romances are relationship stories, it is merely the gender of the characters involved differs from the classic romance tale. The emphasis beyond how they make a commitment to each other at the close of the story is on the Steampunk elements, and I'm sure you know what they are by now without a repeat.

A romance will need to be 50% or more about a couple falling in love and what keeps them apart before they realize they want a future together. Romances are relationship stories and just because you've dropped your romantic couple (or triple) in a Steampunk world doesn't change that.

Let's move on to another category of Steampunk – the Dystopian tale.

The Dystopian Tale

Despite the wonders of science and mechanics during the Industrial Revolution, there was one result that wasn't a giant leap toward the future. In fact, in many ways it was a fallback to the feudal system where serfs were basically slaves owned by the local lord.

The Industrial Revolution created the factory system. Goods that had once been produced by a family out of their home as a cottage industry were now turned out in large quantities using steam powered machines. They were also created with machines built in mass quantities, and new products of all sorts were available in a marketplace hungry for the conveniences they provided.

The people needed to man the machines, the looms, dip the match heads, dig out the coal, etc., became the serfs of progress.

Because conditions were improving as diseases were bested, the population swelled. New enclosure laws turned previously tillable land into pastures for livestock. People from the country streamed towards the cities looking for jobs and a better life than their ancestors had had. Yet, with long hours, wages that were pittances, and more workers available than there were jobs open, once within the factory system, dreams were squashed, living conditions lead to early death and the spread of disease, and prices for housing and other necessities created an unbreakable cycle of hopelessness.

That is the historic dystopian world – one where there appears to be no way out of it.

In Steampunk the dystopian world concept has been embraced by many authors. While the brilliance of the Great Exhibition dazzled the world with an awe inspiring display of scientific and mechanical creations and items brought back from expeditions around the world, the average factory worker crammed an entire family into one room – sometimes more than one generations worth – in the East End slums in London, in the tenements in New

York, Boston, Chicago, Philadelphia, Paris, and other major cities. Children began the 19th century as part of the work force though reformers in the Middle Class pushed through laws to limit both the age and number of hours a child could work. Chances are this hurt the family budget in some families.

Men were always paid more for doing a job than a woman was. Sometimes she received half of a man's wage and children received less than that though they frequently had very dangerous jobs, darting around the machines to check, change or retrieve things. Some jobs relied entirely on a workforce of children, such as the chimney sweeps.

Merely reading Charles Dickens' novels can give us a view of the dystopian life of working children. Dickens himself had been helping to support his family when yet a child. There were numerous schools for thieves, where orphans were taught to be pickpockets by Fagan-like master lifters. Girls began working the streets as prostitutes at young ages, sometimes younger than ten, to either help support parents and siblings, or to simply be able to eat.

A study of crime during the Victorian era will turn up baby farmers where women (many unwed) who needed to work boarded their infants with women who promised to feed, cloth, house, and educate the child for a weekly fee. Frequently the child was dead within a year to a few months, but its biological mother was not informed, and since the factory day didn't allow her time to visit, she kept paying the weekly fee. Women who placed their children with the baby farmers frequently weren't left with enough to survive on themselves and supplemented their income with prostitution to have the meanest food and shelter.

And, in what always seems like the cruelest trick, the strongest among the poor preyed upon their weaker neighbors.

Therefore, whether it is the conditions and low wages paid to workers by those who owned the factories or the people they lived among in the worst parts of the cities, a large segment of Victorian society on both sides of the Atlantic lived in a very dystopian world. In some places they were immigrants (there were large immigrant populations barely getting by in New York, for instance) or locals, as frequently happened in London, Manchester and other industrial cities.

No way out and no hope – that's the dystopian world.

It plays well for Steampunk because it was the creations of the Industrial Age that increased the numbers living in such conditions.

It is the dystopian element that can be seen in stories where someone plans to own the world. Where death stalks the street (aka Jack the Ripper) or the neighborhood is under the thumb of vicious men (The Dead Rabbits gang of New York City's Five Points). Officials take bribes at all levels in these worlds, turn a blind eye to illegal situations.

Dystopian settings can be the result of political takeovers that happened decades to centuries ago, leaving one segment of the population to survive merely as an animal-like workforce, housed in prison conditions or in small communities that barely scrape by on what remains after the state takes what it requires from them. Although it isn't Steampunk, the territories and small communities from which the young contestants for *The Hunger Games* come are dystopian in nature.

The grounding for a dystopian world may well be in historical fact, but you'll need to up the ante in a Steampunk tale and place your main characters in the heart of a depressing world in a depressing situation. And then you'll need to get them out of it. Give them a slim chance, a hope for something better. A reason to use carefully honed talents and possibly even sacrifice themselves...or at least be ready to. If in *The Hunger Games* the surviving teens had been matched against cyborgs with steam powered vehicles and weapons and the society in the city had held Victorian beliefs and mindsets, then it could indeed have been a dystopian Steampunk tale.

If you go back to the origins of science fiction, H.G. Wells' *The Time Machine* has a very dystopian future in it. In *The Anubis Gates*, Tim Powers included a very dystopian Steampunk world beneath the streets of London. Cherie Priest's altered Seattle is a dystopian place.

There is no requirement that dystopian elements be worked into your Steampunk world, but they are a theme that surfaces frequently and in various guises in the genre.

The dystopian tale will be focusing on the dark, the depressing, the hopeless situation of a civilization or a particular part of that civilization. On the persons who keep them in such conditions and why. On resistance fighters determined to change the hopeless situation for the community, and their own along with it as they are of this niche of the population. The dystopian tale is part adventure story, part gothic, so the world building needs to have equally strong doses of hope and determination on the part of the characters. This is the tale that is closest to horror in the genre.

Not everyone wants doom and gloom though. Some readers want a good laugh! Which leads us to...

The Comedic Tale

There are four authors among the Steampunk authors of the late 20th century and early 21st, who really illustrate what is possible when the topic is comedy in Steampunk: Paul di Filippo, Gail Carriger, and the Foglios, Phil and Kaja.

These four could be said to set the standard for mixing alternative Victoriana with slap stick situations and outlandish characters.

Filippo puts a woman-sized newt on the British throne while the queen is off having a bit of fun before settling into her role. Not satisfied, he adds further farce by having the queen's ministers stricken with erotic thoughts and actions when near the uncomplaining newt. The result is a comedy that mixes the fascination of scientists with tinkering with nature, the young Victoria's far from tame diary entries as she contemplated the coming physical side of marriage, and the often times sordid lives of Victorians private lives. "Victoria" is only of the three gems in Filippo's *Steampunk Trilogy*.

Carriger went for the paranormal mix in her Steampunk series, creating a caustic tongued heroine lumbered with air-headed family members, supplied her with a werewolf peer interested in how she tastes (though not when the moon is full), a vampire with the strings of society at his fingertips, and a best friend with the world's worst taste in clothing, then tosses them into a tale fraught with espionage and danger – and a good deal of silliness as well. Carriger's Steampunk world rewrites the structure of society by having weres in charge of the military, and a special enclave of paranormals involved in running the government. The paranormals of Carriger's world are merely one wedge of society in Victoria's realm.

The Foglios are responsible for the graphic novel adventures of the Girl Genius, and the Agatha H. novels spawned from them. This isn't a Victorian world but a Victorian-ish world with many elements appearing to be of German origin – but then so was the

British royal family. Agatha, our Girl Genius, is a whiz at turning out various mechanical objects and goes up against villains who have just as many wonderful whirling, winding, and wheezing machines, some of them robots with strange senses of humor. While adventure is the theme, comedy wiggles its way to the front of every storyline.

Of course, these are just a few of the writers who have worked comedy into their Steampunk storylines.

If you plan to do so as well, look to what history has already supplied for the tweaking:

- Music halls rise to cater to the tastes of the population. Sentimental songs sung by sweet featured women, acrobatics, children who sang and danced, performing animals, and magicians were represented. The fare was always variety and among the acts were always comedians performing skits that featured slap stick, prat falls, and fast-talking prattle. In a story this may not be an act but what they are like normally

- Whether they were the result of a need to fill the music hall stages or the music halls were built to accommodate them, vaudeville and burlesque troupes did regular stops in towns throughout Britain and the U.S. Burlesque had been around since the 1700s featuring comedic plays on the bill. It didn't begin adding the titillation of striptease until the 1860s, and then it was nothing like burlesque later became known for. For the most part, the music hall shows were family fare. Perhaps the racier stuff was featured on the late-night bill. The comedic emphasis was on caricature and parody with skits and songs that could probably be read two different ways

- As mentioned in the character section, traveling circuses begin making the rounds and particularly in the U.S. where P.T. Barnum added the midway with booths, Nature's mistakes were on display for a penny or two in addition to trick riding, wild animals, and clowns. Of course, circuses can be places of terror as well as comedy, but let's stick with the comedy for now and point out that slapstick and mime are prevalent parts of a clown's repertoire.

Naturally, you don't have to include music halls, vaudeville, burlesque or circuses into the mix to supply comedy. There is always wit to keep the ball rolling.

Several 19th century giants are known for their wit: Oscar Wilde, Mark Twain, Abraham Lincoln, and Ambrose Bierce to name a few. Wit is frequently dry, self-depreciating or insulting, but can contain a grain of truth in it.

Another option is the comedy of manners and with the various strictures Victorian middle class and peers appeared to follow in their public life, there is always the possibility of someone tripping up, particularly if they are attempting to live a double life.

It is Steampunk with a comedic edge that characters are often given amusingly impossible (or sometimes Dickensian) names. Things like Thermopoli ffolkes-Smythe, Anthraxia Jones, Thaddeus Timblewelder, Hortense Englecrook or something else equally creative. Don't overdo it and give all characters these sorts of names. Keep it to one or two. Do keep a 19th century feel to all comedic names given, which frequently means grandiose sounding ones.

Comedy in Steampunk can be the slapstick/belly laugh style to the subtle amused curve of the lips or stifled snicker. The choice is up to you.

The comedic storyline will need to have a well-controlled combination of comedic characters and comedic outcomes as well as adventure and possibly a touch of love. Even mystery can find a way to squeeze into this story. Comedy isn't easy to work and needs a strong hand on the reins to hold back some flights of fancy. Here the best idea is to feed comedy through character, and even though what they do results in something to giggle over, it has to be taken seriously as well, particularly if what happens or what is said occurs during a dangerous situation. Not that there need to be any, but if adventure is mixed in, it might be.

The Time Travel Tale

Your character doesn't have to be like the nameless Darwinist adventurer in H.G. Wells' *The Time Machine*, nor be that face changing Gallifreyan who occasionally sits his blue box down in the Victorian world. But he or she can most definitely be a Steampunk hero or heroine or villain to engage in Time Travel in a Steampunk world.

We can give a tip of the bowler to H.G. Wells for making this a very likely story device since his *The Time Machine* is a Victorian/Edwardian tale. Published in 1895 it is early sci-fi and if there is one thing that Steampunk does it is work in the same style stories as were appearing in the period.

The time travel story wasn't exactly new, but *this* type of one was.

It required a machine built by the man traveling within it. It was powered and needed to reach a particular velocity or level to shift forward or backward in time.

Only common sense dictated what Wells did and didn't do to and with his time traveler. You aren't quite as limited.

One of the earliest official Steampunk tales, *The Anubis Gates* by Tim Powers, takes a contemporary college professor back to the past in a time machine. He is inadvertently stranded there and faces dystopian groups, body snatchers, and an enemy who would rather kill him than send him home. He never does get home, by the way.

In Mark Hodder's *Burton and Swinburne* series if a time traveler from the far, far, far distant future hadn't traveled back to 1840 to attempt to keep an ancestor from committing a crime, Hodder's cast wouldn't live in quite as interesting a world as they do in the 1860s.

Some stories supply fake time travel trips only to find that someone among their number is in fact a time traveler.

Characters are welcome to travel from nearly anywhere in history to land in the Industrial Age or step into an alternative or parallel dimension or universe, therefore "time" travel isn't the only out-of-time traveling that can be done.

Whether you wish to use sound technical reasons why the time travel within your story is possible or create time warp "doors" or another device is viable, but before you take this leap consider your audience.

Do the other elements in your story seem to restrict the time travel to "doable" rather than mystical set ups?

There are several ways time travel has been done before (and will be done again) in stories in and out of the Steampunk world.

Wells' hero built a machine and appears to have had required levels it needed to reach to make the journey. And it is a *journey* because he doesn't "leap" into another world, but watches time pass him by, amazed at the changes. It is only when he loses control that the ship/vehicle drops him into a rather prehistoric future.

Hodder's traveler sets dials, controls, and "leaps" in his specially designed suit. If you remember the *Back To The Future* movies, Marty McFly had to get the DeLorian up to a specific speed for the flux capacitor to "leap" him into a different place. In *The Anubis Gates,* Powers does it all with bells, whistles and a flash of light. The coach, horses, and passengers all arrive with a bit of a thump if anything, dematerializing in the present to land in the past, and they have a Cinderella feature built in for they have to be back in the same location by an allotted time to make the leap back to their own time, thus they aren't traveling "in" a time machine but rather are compelled by a "time beam", if you will, one that requires certain elements that are in flux and not always available.

Time travel can take a different direction, too. It can be the result of riffs in time or doorways that open and close at random or at least on a program that appears random.

Nature can have a hand in things. Lighting and storms have long been used as doorways between worlds and a different spot in time is a viable place for a character to find themselves after being struck or caught up in one.

Mysterious or magical entryways can also be used. Following lei lines could result in a shift elsewhere.

Victorians were big on exploring the unknown, if you recall, and that means they'll enter any area where the natives warn them not to go.

Sometimes the trick to building a viable time shift tale (be it time travel, or gateway to another time period) is in considering what will best fit your specific story.

There's only one extremely important question to answer here: *is time travel absolutely required?* Perhaps it's a dimensional shift rather than time travel that suits better. In integrating time travel into the story there must be a *reason* why it is used.

In *The Anubis Gates* the professor from the late 20th century would not be in early Victorian London unless he travels there by time machine.

Without the time travel technology embedded in his suit, the traveler from the distant future in Hodder's stories would not promote chaos in Victorian technology when the 19th century technologists get their hands on that suit and begin making changes that will alter history.

In either case these stories can't be told without the time travel element nor could the changes that do ensue come about without it.

At least in these two books.

It's all in how you put your world together, how you make it sound logical to the reader.

Sometimes that demands technology be involved and sometimes it takes something else.

Shifters, Demons, and Such?

By strict definition a Steampunk story is not one that uses characters who aren't human or aren't human any longer. No beings a spirit like demons or angels or old gods, no members of the Fae or from legend or fairytales like gorgons, grendels, trolls, dwarves, etc.

Does that mean you can't use them? Absolutely not. It's just that you'll be treading the line between Gaslamp Fantasy, which does use them, and Steampunk, which is more science and technology based.

The Parasol Protectorate stories were mentioned earlier as having both werewolf and vampire communities as a normal part of the world and a main character who is pretty much a one of a kind being who wasn't created, simply occurs, and usually because one of their parents was a Soulless being, so it's passed through the natural bloodline.

Many Steampunk tales incorporate revenants/zombies. In many cases, a person becomes a revenant or zombie by being bitten by one of them and the state in which they then live is the result of a virus. If characters are attempting to find a cure for the virus, that fits into a Steampunk scenario as it is science in action.

Because the Spiritualist movement was very big in Victorian times, and not just in England, rather than simply have charlatans running the seances, there might be real communication with those beyond the veil but without a machine or formula to make it possible, the story would not be Steampunk, but merely a historical. Maybe historical horror. Seeing that fake ectoplasm coming out of the medium's mouth or ears or nose or a faux phantasm would freak me out at any rate, and these people didn't have movies with CGI to compare it to.

Drug use was big, and you didn't have to get a pipe in Limehouse or one of the many Chinatowns in North America or Australia, either, to indulge. Reference Sherlock Holmes' use of that 7% solution that he'd shoot up when bored. But George Mann's hero, Sir Maurice Newberry, is not only a user and an addict, he studies the occult and while he ruins his health, sometimes the combination of drugs and occult rituals aids in the Steampunk investigation in his world. To many, occult elements equate to magic that has nothing to do with stage illusions.

The Grimm boys with their collection of peasant folk tales also set the stage for the use of beings and creatures and situations that appear in what we call Fairy Tales. While I would classify the use of these beings as Gaslamp Fantasy, they could merely be part of the cast in a Steampunk tale – if they are involved in technology or science in some way. And where there is a will, there is always a way for the crafty Steampunk writer.

The old gods can have a similar sway as archaeology was really kicking off in this period. No longer was it merely the hobby of the rich who went around collecting odd pieces in their travels, it was becoming a science with many different subsets: Egyptology and Paleontology were big. In *The Anubis Gate*, it's the mysteries of ancient Egypt that get worked into the story. Mummies are big with collectors and have been for decades already. And if there's a curse...well, all hell could break lose. How can the various pantheons shove an immortal finger in your Steampunk pie? Well, don't they visit mortals? Once no longer worshipped, they could get bored. Could start building machines – there is that Antikythera contraption that was found in the 20th century and could be found instead in the 19th century. It could have been made by some bored godling on Olympus, couldn't it? One who could have had it stolen by someone and...well, more than one scenario could be dreamed up for a Steampunk take, couldn't it?

If we've got old gods, why not demons, djinn, angels? Someone could be harnessing them with spells found in recently found, recently translated texts, and giving them physical forms that are either mechanical or biological, right?

And what about a biologist who tinkers with things and comes up with a unicorn, a Pegasus, a gorgon, a minotaur, an Anubis, a dragon...just because, if they ever existed, they are now extinct, doesn't mean they can't be recreated, with either beneficial results or bad ones.

GEARED UP WRITING STEAMPUNK

As long as you keep your Steampunk mantra of *Science* and/or *Technology* and work in a created being (and, you gotta admit, sticking a djinn in something that makes it viciously mobile rather than in a bottle, is definitely a created being), then magic, the Fae, immortal spirits, and beings from legend, are all up for grabs.

Magic Gears

Magic or the occult frequently makes an appearance in Steampunk fiction. However, let's clarify that when the Industrial Age's machines and science and a created being are not a part of the world built in a Victorian story, but magic is a main element, then the tale is a Gaslamp fantasy. Toss in the machines or science and the created being and – bingo – you've got a Steampunk adventure that just happens to include magic or the occult as well. And, yes, I just mentioned that in the section above but we're going to look closer at these elements now.

Real magic can be good or bad, depending on which of your characters are wielding it. Practitioners are sorcerers or wizards, not magicians.

Magicians do stage magic, that is, illusion, but a stage magician might have some other powers to make things disappear, float, materialize. They might have the ability to see things through another's eyes rather than rely on the verbal clues an assistant supplies in a mind reading segment of the act. They may be able to catch a bullet fired at them rather than have it be an illusion. There were a lot of magicians on tour in the Victorian and beyond it. You have the option to have them be illusionists using slight-of-hand and misdirection alone or combine it with something their competition can't match – the *real* magic of a wizard.

Both illusionists and magic practitioners use special words (Abracadabra!), chemistry (smoke screens for illusionists, potions for wizards, witches, sorcerers and sorceresses), and sometimes machines. Stage illusionists have props of all types that they develop to stun and amaze audiences, but magic practitioners could build beings and animate them without the need to power them via winding clockworks, or steam or diesel fueled pistons. Only a sorcerer is likely to be able to create a golem though.

Real magic, in other words, isn't based on devised and practiced deceptions but on power of some sort. It can be based in an old religion's practices – something passed down to apprentices or studied on the sly with the use of those ancient texts that might be found. It could be passed down in a bloodline – frequently seers (Irish or gypsy) and witches inherit abilities even if everyone in the family doesn't have the gift.

A long life or immortality is frequently a plus for members of a magically gifted family, but it can also be the result of a potion or a thing created in an alchemist's lair. The Philosopher's (or Sorcerer's) Stone was a project attempted by many medieval and renaissance alchemists, but success was supposedly only granted to the legendary Nicolas Flamel. Although in some fiction the Philosopher's Stone grants immortality, other sources claim it was used to turn base metal into silver or gold. It was the Elixir of Life that pushed the inevitability of death aside. The historical Flamel lived into his 80s, dying in the early 1400s in Paris, but the legendary Flamel was reportedly still active and kicking centuries later. Supposedly he found a copy of the *Book of Abramelin the Mage*, a Jewish magic text, and managed to translate its secrets from Hebrew. The creation of golems is frequently associated with Jewish magicians or mystics, the recipe for one nearly replicating the creation of Adam in *Genesis*: create a body from mud and insert one of the secret names of God (written in Hebrew on a scrap of paper, in this case) to activate. Golems usually lack the ability to speak but are difficult to stop as they continue to reassemble. Imagine one made of brass, copper and iron that could do whatever the character in your Steampunk world who imbued it with life wished.

Victor Frankenstein's monster is also viewed by some as a golem, but one that can speak. It comes off far more articulate and conniving in Mary Shelley's tale than it ever does on the big screen.

The ancient Egyptians are well known for using magic, though rather than create golems they enchanted mummies to protect the remains and treasures of a buried king or queen or highly placed priest or official. Mummies, after all, are only "activated" by the arrival of someone who doesn't belong in the tomb. Although the "curse of the mummy" that newspapermen reported culled those who opened King Tut's tomb in the 1920s, Egyptology was big during the 19th century and few curses appear to have felled expedition members. The Rosetta Stone had been found by Napoleon's troops in

Egypt in 1799 and snagged by the British in 1801. It, if you remember your history, was instrumental in allowing scholars to finally translate the hieroglyphics of the old kingdoms. Archaeology wasn't a science yet, though by the turn of the century Flinders Petrie was founding the modern system used at dig sites today. Earlier than that amateurs waded in to dig for ancient treasures, and occasionally stumbled into traps set by the builders to deter grave robbers. Ahh, the adventures your characters could have if they encounter old magic "trip-wires". (Consider the variety of devious traps that Indiana Jones has to get past at the start of *Raiders of the Lost Ark* as these sorts of ancient security technology systems.)

Arabia is also an ancient land with myths to tap. Scheherazade spun tales that included djinns in lamps who granted a specific number of wishes, of flying carpets, and thieves' caves that could only be entered using a magic word – "Sesame." There are no doubt other stories available to be tapped for magical qualities and a possible quest for riches or lost cities. Naturally we'll be taking along the latest in Steam tech weapons.

While the wonders of ancient Egypt had been in European sight for centuries, those of the lost empires of South American and Mexico had not been. Oh, sure, the Spanish had stomped on Aztecs and Incas back in the 1500s, and the Jesuits probably thought they'd snagged and destroyed (or shipped back to the Vatican) any Codexes that might serve as magical text books, but no one had stumbled across the ruins left behind by the Toltecs, Olmecs, or the Mayan until the first came to light in the 1830s. With the Jesuits no longer present, any texts found were more likely to survive – not that they'd make it into publicly accessible libraries. There could be secrets galore in those texts and if one of your characters got their hands on it...well, the magic of these ancients could be whatever you wish to make it.

Different sorts of magic can be outsourced from India, Africa, the jungles of Siam (modern Thailand) and the surrounding countries, from the Tibetan and Himalayan highlands, from the Aboriginals of Australia, New Zealand, Guinea, and other South Pacific spots, and on up into Asia with the Moguls, the Cossacks, the Chinese, Japanese and Korean areas. There are always legends to tap, some tied to religions (like those Jewish golems) or ancient pantheons.

Even the Greeks and Romans have soothsayers and magic practitioners. Oddly enough, they even had "vending machines" where a coin could be dropped in to get a prediction from a soothsayer way back then, too.

More to the era of our Steampunk stories though are the Gypsies, whether they are considered formerly ousted Egyptians or Romanian ("Roms"), they travel in caravans, are outsiders no matter where they go, are fortune tellers, have a magical way with horses, and sell potions to cure ills or make someone fall in love with the purchaser. They can also level curses on people, possessions (from animals to buildings to wagons, tools, furniture...you name it), or on families for generations.

Witches are also known for doing this, but then many considered the gypsies who did any of these things witches.

Those using *real* magic, as opposed to illusion, then could be identified as creating potions, telling fortunes, leveling curses, animating inanimate (or dead in the case of mummies) beings or objects (those carpets), and using terms that activate something ("abracadabra", "sesame", or written words in an ancient language).

The Occult

The Occult is slightly different because it usually involves drawing power from evil supernatural sources to do magic. Trafficking with demons, devils, imps, some of the old gods with nasty reputations.

One of the groups that falls into the Occult rather than merely Magical are those who practice Voodoo. They also have fortune tellers, level curses, make potions, and reanimate the dead into zombies (though there are also *living* zombies, that is people who appear to be zombies but aren't dead). Control is accomplished through a version of Mesmerism and/or snake venom. Killing from a distance – or causing pain – is accomplished through the construction of a Voodoo doll that has something physical of the person it resembles used in the creation. It could be a single hair.

The Occult also brings in the ability to talk to the dead (séances were hugely popular in the 19th century, remember?), but it can include possession, poltergeist activity, or mind control that isn't entirely mesmerically achieved.

With Occult magic something is traded or bargained to a demonic being of some sort to gain something, usually mastery of something. Beside this level of power, *real* magic is tame. And the practitioner only thinks they are in control. The dark being called is playing them, in other words.

Far more drawing of pentagrams is likely in the Occult province. Any symbols used will be so obscure and secret that only a few will have knowledge of them unlike with those used in *real* magic, which tend to be in Latin or an ancient version of another still spoken language. The language of the Occult was never spoken other than to evoke a being of power.

Runes can also be used and tattoos infused with spells.

The Occult frequently surfaces in urban fantasy tales, if you need a comparison in another genre.

There are far more opportunities for using *real* magic or illusion in a Steampunk world, but the Occult certainly has a place as well. I already mentioned that in George Mann's Newberry and Hobbs Steampunk world, Sir Maurice is an expert in the occult and, much to the despair of Miss Hobbs, has drawn his share of pentagrams, obscure symbols, and chanted himself into dangerous situations. If Sherlock Holmes turned his mind to the Occult, rather than identifying all manner of tobacco ash, his fixation would be similar. The Victorian men of science could be fanatical when it came to their pet projects.

The fact that either magic of illusion can supply a created being for Steampunk makes magic of any sort a viable element to use.

The unknown did so tantalize Victorians.

Magic or the Occult isn't a requirement, but then Steampunk has but a few requirements. One of those is changing history to fit a new model.

Some might say, mangling it.

Mangling History

Mangling history is perhaps the most fun a writer can have in choosing to write Steampunk. This is the way to do it:

> **Pick one event and change the outcome
> and then recreate everything
> that would happen in society
> – in history –
> as a result of this change**

Before you can change an event, you need to know what happened in history to begin with. While it is possible to go back a century or more before the 19th century, it makes far more sense to stick with things that did take place during the 19th century as that will keep the "what if-ing" under control and more to the point for a Steampunk tale.

There are political events that could be changed. For instance, if George IV had had a legitimate son who survived to inherit the crown rather than a daughter who died in 1817, then when George himself died in 1830 his brother would not have succeeded him, and been succeeded in turn by the 18 year old Victoria a few years later. With a king who might also have had a son to follow him, Victoria would remain a minor royal and even if she did wed her cousin Albert of Saxe-Coburg and Gotha, neither would have had influence on the way society behaved to the extent they did as Queen and Consort.

On the other hand, if Victoria hadn't wed Albert but had married a man with entirely difference strengths and weaknesses than Albert had, things would have played out differently. Change Vicky's groom and attitudes toward several things change – if she follows his lead as she did with Albert, that is.

She could also follow Elizabeth I's example and merely flirt with the idea that she would choose a husband but never do so.

This illustrates only three ways that things could change related to the throne. There are also numerous politicians who could have their lives rearranged, lengthened, or ended. If Robert Peel hadn't been prime minister and pushed through police reform there would be no Scotland Yard and a lot of minor crimes would have continued to merit the death sentence with him unavailable to get them off the books. Give the Irish free rule early in the century and you wipe out the Fenian terrorist activities as well as a need for the Irish Special Branch at the Yard.

More than one Steampunk set up has had Britain squashing the colonial uprising in America which results in there being no United States.

Let's leave the political jockeying and look at the mechanical side of things.

We've probably all heard that as the century turned from 19th to 20th Henry Ford invented the assembly line. At least he certainly is remembered for the number of Model Ts his factory could turn out using that system. But in 1853 "The Long Shop" was turning out portable steam engines in Richard Garrett & Sons' Suffolk shop in much the same way. What if the assembly line went into action far earlier? Considering the workers at Ford's plant were soon bored and frustrated by doing the same action repeatedly, it's a perfect set up for a dystopian set up. Today we have robotics doing much of the repetitive work but in the early Industrial Age the idea of wasting machinery on such jobs might appear illogical since a human workforce was plentiful and cheap. Perhaps robots become the overseers. Wonder how Luddites would take to that?

The same thing can be done with scientific discoveries – not in putting robots in charge, but in changing when things happen or who makes the discovery and what they do with it. A lot of the things we take for granted today were discovered in the 19th and early 20th century. Astronomically, asteroids, Neptune and the Transit of Venus came to light. Medically, chloroform and X-rays and radiation to kill cancer cells. Darwin formulated the evolution theories; Freud concentrated on the mind. Einstein dreamed up a different theorem in dealing with gravity: $E=mc^2$. Babbage had sketched out a plan for a "difference engine", which is considered the first computer – or would be if it had been built outside of fiction (reference *The Difference Engine* by Gibson and Sterling, 1990).

Public works projects such as the sewers of Paris (1855) and London (1859-1865), the London Underground (first section opened in 1863), New York's Subway in 1904 and the elevated rails that began operation in 1869, are just a few of them. Do the job at an earlier time, a later time, not at all, or differently and you've altered history for the characters in your Steampunk story.

All parts of society can be affected when something is discovered, or men of equal caliber dream up improvements on each other's inventions. The Voltage Wars between Edison and Tesla "began" when Tesla's method of alternating current came up against Edison's contracts with various cities. Edison's laboratory teams turned out all sorts of conveniences and entertainment for his customers: light bulbs, sound recording devices, moving pictures, etc. Photography was the big thing from the 1830s for tintypes on through the silent movies of the early 20th century. No reason you can't speed up progress to turn Lilly Langtry into a cinema star in the first "talkie". One of the fastest growing appliance needs from the late 1870s onwards were telephones, and not just in the U.S. Victoria had one installed the year after Mr. Bell visited her. Just think what you could do with his invention! Or with the telegraph! The trans-Atlantic cable was successfully laid during this period as well.

The Wright Brothers were among the many working on manned motorized flying machines if you recall from the character chapter. When combined with the interest in astronomy, it certainly leads to the early science fiction stories of journeys to Mars and the Moon. And why not? Explorers were heading out into the wilds around the world and coming back with previously unheard-of marvels. Just because things weren't unearthed or discovered historically is no reason why they can't appear as a normal part of your Steampunk world if you set things up to make them fairly logical.

Among the things being improved upon, don't overlook weaponry. Not only did rifling of barrels and multi-shot pistols make appearances, there was a relay system with steam powered ships at sea delivering troops and supplies to railroads that moved them on to various warfronts inland. After 1910 small aircraft entered the arsenals of warring nations, as did diesel powered conveyances.

There are machines and advancements being made in rapid succession throughout the 1800s, particularly after 1830, in Britain, the United States and Europe. All it takes is for you to have the glimmer of an idea and then a plunge into research related to that glimmer to begin building both a specialized Steampunk world and Steampunk storyline.

There is no rule on how many things a writer needs to change, or how few. It depends on the vision dancing in your mind.

Some things should not change though. The reason is that a Steampunk world should invoke the look and feel of the historic 19th and early 20th century. Steampunk is alternative historical fiction, so the historical needs a strong visual representation.

Things that should stay much the way they were are:

The Clothing

Men will have wool suits, weskits, ties or ascots, top hats, bowlers or felt hats with brims or tweed "newsboy" style caps if they are operating out of a city. The "skirts" of frock coats recede over time to the shorter, box jacket. Edward, Prince of Wales, popularized what became the tuxedo for formal wear. Find photographs taken of workers throughout the 19th century and early 20th and the weskits, ties and hats will be in evidence even if jackets have been removed and shirt sleeves turned back while tinkering with machines.

Women will have long skirts, but the style of their gowns will change with the decade. Bustles came and went and returned, hats were always worn when leaving the house and not necessarily taken off while visiting friends. Should your female characters be mechanics they might don long leather aprons (some of the men may wear these as well) or be very daring and wear trousers or bloomers. Corsets, of course, are one of the things associated with Steampunk heroines. Be aware that in many places, a woman wearing men's clothing could be arrested and jailed. Ditto a man in female attire. Crossdressing was definitely frowned upon but that didn't stop people from donning what they pleased. And, if you are a fan of Conan Doyle's Sherlock Holmes, you might have read a story where Holmes disguised himself as a woman when he needed a covert identity during an investigation.

Gloves will be worn by the upper class of both sexes. Canes are in evidence among the gentlemen but also are affected by some ladies. Face hair for men changed with the decade as well, so finding photographs taken near the year chosen for the story will be an excellent guide. The same works for women's hair and hats, which can go from small to large and befrilled with feathers, ribbons, netting, and even feature taxidermied avians depending on the year.

And we can't forget those brass goggles, though in reality they would have appeared only once the speed of diesel vehicles and aircraft made their historical appearance. If your characters will have transportation that would cause their eyes to water due to the wind in their face, by all means, hand them a pair of goggles. Otherwise, goggles might be worn by mechanics welding the bits and pieces of their creations together.

Transportation

Although there is steam power, it hasn't totally replaced the horse yet on the streets. Hansom cabs are associated with London but because they were extremely maneuverable and required only one horse, they also showed up in New York City and Paris. Most large deliveries will still be made by huge wagons drawn by two or more horses. In the American West (and possibly Australia and Canada) oxen and mules will be more in evidence when hauling is required. Be careful if you attempt to hitch a water buffalo up in India though. It might be someone's ancestor.

Long distances can be traveled by train but only if the tracks have been laid. In Britain, the tracks went down in all directions in fairly rapid succession. The more rural the area, the less likely it was to have a locomotive chug into town, particularly in the American West and even in the Southern states. In New England where manufacturing was rampant, the rails radiated out to various markets. The British laid rails in India to make it easier to deliver troops and supplies to their outposts but those are limited. In the U.S., the first track to connect one side of the continent to the other was completed in 1869. The longest railroad in the world is still the

Trans-Siberian, built from 1891 to 1916, and dealing with tigers in some areas was one of the "adventures" workers had to deal with. Train travel is a given for the period, though you can always tinker with the type and speed.

Canals were the precursors of the rails in Britain but many of the American canal systems were being dug at nearly the same time as the rail lines were being laid. Stagecoaches were still necessary to make connections to many places. Even in a specifically constructed Steampunk world there should be destinations that progress hasn't reached yet in regard to transport, but your characters could fix that.

Even though, in building a Steampunk world, new methods of transport will no doubt materialize, they will still be fairly "newfangled" devices and be jockeying for space on the roads with the historic modes of transport. The skies will be fairly clear since only balloons were plying the area above ground level unless you've gone into major dirigible manufacturing prior to their historical appearance in the heavens.

The Society
Part of Steampunk's flavor is in the class system and the *morés* of those in a position of power. There are the extremely rich on both sides of the Atlantic, but these fortunes are frequently self-made rather than inherited along with titles. Money, as noted earlier, was being made by industrialists.

The Astor family of New York built on wealth acquired through the fur trade in the early 1800s, but the Rockefellers' money came from oil, the Vanderbilts' from a steamboat monopoly then railroads. These are just a few of the American elite families.

Where Victoria's notions held sway in Britain, it was matriarchs like Mrs. Astor who made the rules in New York.

The Middle Class was rising in wealth on both sides of the ocean and as they tended to be tied more closely to religious affiliations than the upper crust, morals were just as important as manners, who you knew and who you associated with. More zealous missionary efforts grow from the involvement at this level, but we can include the suffragette and temperance movements as related to these, as well. People are more educated than their ancestors but are very much in sync with the ideals linked to Victoria even if she isn't the visible head of their government. There will be nationality differences, of course, with the British appearing more strait-laced than the French, the Germans being more militaristic and the Americans (and probably the Australians and Canadians) considered rather brash sorts.

The worker class, the servants, and the poor also remain intact historically. Tinkering with one group in a specific area is possible but changing the way things are on a large scale from what they were historically will destroy part of what makes a Steampunk world indelibly Victorian.

Even if set in an alternate or parallel universe, on a distant planet or in the future, it is the things that the Victorians and their nearest neighbors held dear that are important to keep.

Beyond the visuals of costume, transportation, and the *mores* of society, change is possible.

One possible way to look at things is to change something in more than one category when building your Steampunk world. Consider these:

- A change in the makeup of the government. Gail Carriger turned over certain elements of government to groups of paranormals. Or you can let a different side win in a war or at the elections

- Change something about the way a certain segment of the population lives. To cut down on crime in the East End of London, turn the entire section into a walled prison or to do the same thing in New York City, build a floating prison city or transport all incoming immigrants to Texas and the New Mexico Territory. If you can dream it up, you can make it work. And there were many who were unhappy about the number of immigrants arriving, so there is a built-in historical segment of the population who would be all for these sort of solutions

- There are many religious movements in the U.S. that set up their own communities. The Mormons are merely one of these. There are similar missionary movements in Britain. The Spiritualist and temperance movements were on similar wave lengths – ones where they believed they are right, and others should jump on the bandwagon. Corrupt or invent a similar movement for your story

- Change, recreate or invent something earlier than it was done historically. The same applies to scientific finds. In Scott Westerfeld's series he jumped on the idea of creating biologicals to his own designs with early gene splicing

- Consider more than merely the mechanical advances and look to the architectural. Make it possible to build skyscrapers earlier than 1885; cut down on city pollution by enclosing the wealthier part of the city under a glass dome; create subterranean or underwater communities

- Look at what there was and what could grow from it in your world. Also look to what has been created in the world of fiction, not merely modern Steampunk novels and short stories, but in Victorian and Edwardian era tales. Conan Doyle gave Holmes a master criminal to confront and best in Moriarty. Perhaps your characters have a mysterious nemesis. Holmes also made use of boys who could roam the streets and gather intelligence for him. The men of the Sûreté and the Yard's Special Branch donned disguises and did undercover work against thieves, murderers, and terrorists. All of these are viable Steampunk situations

But until you know what did happen, what life was like, deciding on what to augment or adapt or adopt or change can't be accomplished. If you aren't familiar with a locale or what things were like in a particular decade, head to the Internet, to the library, to the host of books that have been written or republished from the period. Look at maps of the cities, of the rail lines. Discover what was going on politically, in the war office, what happened to returning soldiers, what sent the people of various nations to immigrate into the cities, into adjacent countries or across the seas to distant lands. Find out how well Darwin's theories were received, or Freud's, or how controversy arose about the age of the planet between those who thought the Bible told it all and what the new sciences were insisting was the truth.

History holds a wealth of ideas to use, to corrupt to your own devices. It also can inspire new spurts of brilliance when building either your Steampunk world or your Steampunk plot.

World and Plot Building

To better see how this can all come together, let's return to that scenario with the family headed to Mars and what the Steampunk world they live in – before they head to Mars – is like.

The first thing we need to do is flesh out who these people are – start with the basics and then build from there.

The father is the respected scientist. Because he likely had the more classical education when he was at school, he might spout Cicero or other ancient philosophers as an element of his personality, which would suit a gentleman of the period on either side of the Atlantic.

Things to decide are whether he has a teaching position at a university, and if so whether a real university should be used, or one should be invented. In America, M.I.T. opened its doors shortly before the Gilded Age and has the right curriculum with an emphasis on engineering, chemistry and other course work that is more in sync with the needs of invention. If the story uses the American East Coast – Boston – as the home base, this story isn't Victorian, and it isn't Weird West but is Weird Urban East. Lacking the podium and connections of the Royal Society, either a similar sort of historical organization can be found, or one could be created. Inventing one that can be crafted to the story's needs might allow the building of a very visually Steampunk college and "club" of scientific men and women.

Obviously, the scientist will be derided by most of his colleagues who find his ideas and the viability of his being able to travel to Mars impossible. The man's a crackpot as far as his peers are concerned. He could point out other inventors or men of science who were also considered so and mention improvements now taken for granted in Boston. And there's no reason why those he mentions can't be fictional and their creations things that are only taken for granted in this particular Steampunk world.

Because we need someone to believe in him at least one person will step forward to fund the expedition, to finance the journey, but it might turn out that they have ulterior motives. In fact, they *should* have them. Enthusiastic and helpful on the surface but plotting to take advantage of or grab control of the scientist's creation and any resources he discovers on Mars. Whether it is those forests he mistakenly believes exist or something better, like precious metals, gemstones, or something else, this helpful villain is probably necessary to this plot.

In dreaming up this idea originally the scientist was gifted with a wife and daughter who were going to accompany him on the journey. If the daughter is equally brilliant in the lab and in her early twenties or a student at M.I.T., we can judge that her father is in his fifties and her mother possibly in her late forties. A decision will need to be made on whether the mother is more interested in getting her daughter married or is of a scientific bent as well. If she's more interested in domesticity, she either has to be used by the helpful nemesis or conveniently dropped from the cast (cholera or consumption are handy historical ways to eliminate her).

Because it would be more interesting to have something go wrong and the scientist and whoever accompanies him be stranded on Mars, there will need to be a stalwart rival who has the wherewithal to go to the rescue. There will need to be a reason why our scientist is getting the jump on him in the space race to Mars. Perhaps he has been concentrating on the Moon as a more viable first step. Perhaps he has been working on time jumps to increase the speed of trips to off-Earth locations. Perhaps his lab suffered a disaster when he refused to do business with the fellow so helpfully supplying the funds for the Mars mission.

Part of this Steampunk world will need to concentrate on the space craft itself, what it looks like inside, how they will deal with the lack of gravity, with supplying sufficient oxygen. What sort of suits they will wear when stepping forth on the surface of Mars. The sort that divers used for underwater salvage certainly can serve as a model, but they'll need to be altered for space travel and visits to planets lacking sufficient oxygen. Finding out what *was* known about Mars in the decade chosen for the story is a great starting spot to build this element of the story's world.

Because keeping the Victorian look that was popular in homes on both sides of the Atlantic is important, let's make the interior of the space vehicle part ship's cabin and part comfy parlor. Portholes with multi-pane construction like modern energy efficient windows have but with more layers. Bunks built into niches with cocoon like blankets that are affixed to the sides and keep the sleeper from floating away from the mattress. Perhaps heavy drapes that can be drawn over the niche to give the sleeper privacy. Overstuffed armchairs with seat belts, though ottomans that can be on tethers allowing the seated person to prop their feet up at any angle they wish. A mock fireplace that is fed by heat from the steam engine. Some source of lighting will be needed but the use of flame would be unadvisable since it would consume oxygen, and with that in mind, perhaps the ship itself needs something different than a steam engine to power it – boilers do require flames after all. Maybe it is a giant clockwork and has a turnstile to wind it. Some thought will be necessary as well as research into using natural phosphorescent materials for lighting.

There should be wheels, gears, tubes, and pipes in evidence, though perhaps viewed through windowed trapdoors in the ceiling. There will also need to be a ladder to reach machinery above and below (where the boilers – or clockworks – and fuel or oil for the gears is stored) – one of those corkscrew iron staircases would look right. Meals will need to be worked out – how to make them and keep the ingredients from floating around the cabin – but if possible, they should be served on hand painted delicate china.

The daughter will wear skirts until she climbs inside the ship where trousers will avail her better. To complete her transformation, she should exchange her corset for a weskit. Perhaps have a newsboy cap to bundle her hair beneath though she'll need her hairpins to keep those silky locks in place. The pins might come in handy as weapons somewhere in the story, or to fix something.

The control panel will obviously be a massive board of dials with needles that swing back and forth giving readouts from the various machines that power the ship. There will need to be some sort of transmission system that is used briefly, perhaps once a week, to assure those back on Earth that all is well or, when it becomes necessary, to send out that S.O.S.

That's the ship. What's it look like back on Earth?

Obviously, a lot of Boston will remain the same. The scientist's lab and building where he builds and launches his ship from will need to be designed, but it will likely have much the same look as the inside of the ship...the wheels, gears, etc. The house will be a comfortable Gilded Age home though it might be augmented with some household appliances that either the scientist or the daughter designed and built.

A map of Boston will come in handy for mentioning neighborhoods, historical buildings, street names, businesses or the names of theatres, shops or whatever else might be needed though they can be invented, too. The topography can be snagged from a search for photographs from the year or near the year being cited for the story. Deciding what Steampunk enhancements could be made to the look of Boston itself is part of the fun.

All that is left is to design a Steampunk Martian world, invent a system of propulsion that appears to make sense, and to dream up the final details of the plot.

This is a fairly simple set up because the story plays out more on the ship and in the labs than it does in Boston itself. Some authors keep quite a lot of history intact while others throw themselves into the creation of their Steampunk worlds. Part of the way they accomplish this is by creating biologicals and mechanicals that do things like street maintenance or become public transportation on land or in the skies – things seen every day and taken for granted.

The idea of changing the political situation by altering a historical personage's life has already been tossed out. Once what was has been changed, a writer needs to look at all aspects of life that that person might have had an influence in. Victoria, of course, is a major one, but so too would be that of a mechanic, engineer, scientist, diplomat, explorer, etc.

Some things will be simple: what if the British had never imported tea? What would they be drinking in vast quantities? Having tea is so identifiably British.

What if the cholera epidemics in the cities had decimated them rather than lead to improvements in sewer and water treatment systems?

What if the Luddites had carried the day and rather than the Industrial Revolution leading to the numerous discoveries and inventions, manufacturing had retreated back to the cottage craft system with laws passed to limit, restrict or even forbid certain types of advancements from ever being made? At least, in Britain. The rest of the world might have chugged on ahead and inaugurated the Industrial Revolution on the soil of a different nation.

The Steampunk world you build can be an improvement on the historical one or it can retreat into dystopian hell for part of the population. It's all up to you.

But If You Don't Have Any Ideas For A Story...

Let's say you really haven't the first glimmer of an idea for a story and need inspiration. Research can come to your rescue!

For the sake of illustration, let's pick a year. How about 1839.

We'll start with *The Timetables of History: A Horizontal Linkage of People and Events* by Bernard Grun. *Timetables* tells us that in 1839 the First Opium War broke out between Britain and China, Edgar Allan Poe's "The Fall of the House of Usher" was published, John Lloyd Stephens rediscovered and examined the antiquities of the ancient Mayans in Central America, Mendelssohn conducted Schubert's Symphony in C major, Charles Goodyear discovered the process of "vulcanization" making the commercial use of rubber possible, the metallic element lanthanum and the ozone were both discovered, the theory of cell-growth was formulated, the first electric clock was built, Abner Doubleday laid out the first baseball field and conducted the first baseball game ever played, the first bicycle was constructed, Cunard got in the shipping business, the First Grand National (that's a horse race) was run at Aintree, England, Prussia restricted juvenile labor to a maximum of 10 hours a day, and W.H. Fox Talbot claimed that he obtained successes with his photographic experiments before Daguerre and communicates the results to the Royal Society.

There's some fodder here, but for more options, let's head for *The Illustrated History of the 19th Century*. This supplies a month-by-month and year-by-year list of events, discoveries, etc. to work with and supplies pictures, drawings, paintings, daguerreotypes, and photographs. The benefit here is learning that the Opium War broke out November 10th. It adds that Poe headed to Philadelphia to edit *Burton's Gentleman's Magazine*, that the first commercial production of an artificial fertilizer was applied to a turnip crop with "spectacular results," that Charles Darwin's *Beagle* Diaries were published (and no they weren't about the antics of his dogs), an English photographer was the first to successfully reduce the size of a paper document on film thus inventing the concept of storing information on microfilm, an abortion law was passed in the United Kingdom making it a three year prison worthy offense, two ships headed out in an effort to reach the Magnetic South Pole, the British were also at war in Afghanistan, and the American West was opened for settlement and further exploration.

If we decide to set this Steampunk tale in 1839, we've already got a lot of things that are worthy of inclusion here. A bit of further, more detailed or in-depth research for things we might want to freeze in their historical place and a half-cup of imagination could supply quite a bit to work with here.

The First Temptation

How's this: Our hero has just watched or participated in the very first baseball game ever played, but he needs to be en route to England for undisclosed reasons (he could be a spy! Either governmental or industrial, which would work well here). Tucking either the magazine in which "The Fall of the House of Usher" was published, or the current copy of *Burton's Gentleman's Magazine* under his arm, he manages to get passage on a ship partially owned by a fellow named Cunard who has big dreams. They fall into a discussion of Darwin's finds whilst aboard the sailing ship, *The Beagle*, and Cunard mentions the war in Afghanistan and how he's heard relations in China will soon disrupt the Opium Trade, damn shame, not that he agrees with that sort of thing. Our hero says he's tempted to find adventure in the West, shake a few Sioux or Blackfoot hands, but he's heard there are some rather mysterious gold items being unearthed in the South American jungles, some lost civilization or some such. Upon docking in Liverpool, our hero really gets down to business. Seems there is some deranged genius who intends to hold the world for ransom – if he doesn't get oodles and oodles of cash (the technical term for it, of course) he's going to destroy the ozone and suck all the oxygen from the atmosphere. And the plans for the machine he has built to do the evil deed are stored on a series of photographic cells (those infant microfiche thingies). However, to complicate things the hero has to attend the Grand National and it is there he discovers someone else is out to get our evil genius, a girl out for revenge because the villain forced her sister to get an abortion or perform one and now she's on trial and will soon be headed to prison for three years and what with her sad health – consumption, you know – she'll never survive the ordeal!

Hey, have we got a possible story going here, or what? And all we've done is work with really basic information from sources that gave us just the highlights.

But wait! We left some of the data out! We never made it to the South Pole, though isn't it one of those spots where the ozone went holey in modern times? Could that early bicycle be used to create/generate electricity for the electric clock that could set off the destructo machine? Mendelssohn didn't get to conduct the orchestra; Goodyear's rubber didn't get used...but maybe it could be in the ozone eater? And if Mendelssohn instigates a really BIG crescendo...? What the heck is lanthanum, and could it be used to destroy the world in our scenario? Perhaps when mixed with the fertilizer that grew that awesome turnip? Or is one of those turnips just the right size to jam the giant steam powered Destructo the Ozone Eater machine? And how could all of this be related to the theory of cell growth? Hmm, there should be a way. Our evil genius is probably ticked off that children in Prussia, where he grew up, now work shorter hours than he ever did, and Fox Talbot is lying about his own experiments predating Daguerre's because *he* (our evil genius, not Fox Talbot) was the one who hired Daguerre to front his own success when it comes to the photographic process.

Now, if we were writing a graphic novel or Agatha H story like one from the pens of Phil and Kaja Foglio all of this just might be kept, but that's not the goal, so it's time to rein in the imagination and narrow in on the type of story that is more manageable.

Besides, we're still missing something – a created being.

The Doable Schematic

Let's morph our hero into an editor who is put in a spot by his boss and required to go visit one of the publisher's old school mates who has an idea for a book about his observations during a voyage to the South Seas. Hero is thinking cannibals, scantily clothed native girls, and an adventure on a nearly deserted island. The new *Robinson Crusoe*, he thinks, bound to be a best seller. Then he meets the would-be author, Charles Darwin, and is bored to distraction by what the fellow wants to fill the pages of his book with. Wants to work in the name of the ship he was on, *The Beagle*, and just use the notes he made in his diary for the text. Hero sees his career ship sinking and suggests Darwin shove the diary away as an oddity his grandchildren might find interesting decades down the road. If Darwin seriously wants to make money in the publishing business, he should write a book about dogs. The English are mad about dogs, he says. "And look, you've got a Beagle puppy in the yard. Write a chronicle of its antics for a year, talk about training it, how those big brown eyes have you forgiving it for chewing your slippers, stuff like that. We can call it *The Beagle Diaries* and turn a decent bit of coin." As Mrs. Darwin is all for it, Charles shakes hands on the deal and the hero says he'll be back in a year for the manuscript.

His boss is happy with the way things turned out as he didn't think a dry scientific sounding book would do their bottom line much good either. Has a new assignment for our hero. Wants him to head for America and snap up some combination poet-short story spinner named Edgar Allan Poe. Hands him a copy of "The Fall of the House of Usher." Hero agrees this guy needs to be under contract to them and promises to get the deal sealed up. On board the ship he finds a group of scientists off to plunder the wealth of the newly discovered Mayan ruins. One has his attractive daughter along to act as his secretary and photographer and she's come up with a humdinger of a new type of camera (either borrowed from the future or designed to fit the bill here). Hero is smitten and when the ship docks hastily gets Poe's signature on the dotted line then dashes off a proposal to his boss about following the Mayan research group on their journey because he thinks a book of photographs of the temples, artifacts, gentlemen adventurers and natives would be of interest to the almost reading public for display in their parlors. Rather than wait for an answer (the transatlantic cable hasn't been successfully laid yet historically) he does a Phineas Fogg type trip across country to meet the scientists ship at their last port of call on American soil before heading for the jungle.

Let's drop in the idea of the Mayan civilization actually having been built around a group of visitors from off planet, toss in some mummies that are partly mechanical and dangerous so that the members of the scientific group begin to get whittled away until only our hero, the girl with the camera and dark room, and her father are the only ones to get out alive.

Still a lot to plan, but we've changed Darwin's life and Poe's, will be able to take some cutting edge vehicles in the race across country to catch the ship, and have those Created Beings present and dangerous in the tunnels beneath the pyramid structure the team begins excavating.

This is a doable, moderate level Steampunk story with a bit of comedy and romance as well as danger and adventure mixed in.

Of course, it's also possible to take the same historical elements and spin an entirely different tale.

Create A Being

The one thing we haven't done yet that is a Steampunk requirement is create a being.

Not everyone in the Steampunk writing world believes this is a necessary component, but if you drowned yourself in volume after volume of published Steampunk fiction, the one thing that is repeated even more than goggles, corsets, and airships, is a being.

Could be that they are thinking "sentient" being and I'm expanding it to *"seemingly* sentient" being. In either case the new "construct" was "built" by man in some manner (via work in a lab, through magic, or via a bite from a being that *used* to be human), which is really the basis of any Steampunk creation, sentient or non-sentient.

A sentient being can, of course, think for itself, but a *seemingly* sentient being only appears to be doing so via its programming or gear configuration. Frankenstein's monster is a sentient being but the automaton in the movie *Hugo* only appears to be capable of communicating with him to young Hugo at first.

Whether you are thinking sentient or seemingly sentient, the variety of created being that can be constructed is wide ranging.

Sometimes it's a total biological, as Westerfeld's Darwinists specialize in building with gene splicing. More often it is mechanical, like a clockwork or steam powered robot. It can also be part man or animal and part mechanical. It can be as simple as an amputee being supplied with a mechanical limb, or it can be a $100,000 man (what the 19th century price tag for a bionic man might be).

Early androids, cloning, specific cross-breeding to enhance or augment an already existing species, horrific experimentation (Frankenstein's monster could qualify here but so could anyone who was a whole person until a mad scientist began slicing and dicing and making adjustments to them), are all viable. If you can come up with a logical reason why dinosaurs or mammoths could be reanimated (perhaps a cryogenic tie-in) or unicorns, gryphons or dragons recreated, then you have sentient creatures that are no longer natural to the 19th century environment but that definitely meet the criteria of a created being.

Beings can be created via *real* magic (as opposed to *un*real magic which is stage illusion). As mentioned earlier, golems, homunculi, mummies and certain sorts of zombies fill this category. A bite from a vampire or werewolf, and – *voilà!* – we have a created sentient being without going to the trouble of using biology or mechanics.

Possession by an evil spirit creates something that isn't normal as well. Anything that can transfer itself into a different body – a body snatcher as opposed to a shape shifter – has changed form, too.

Anyone who created a potion to alter themselves in some manner, be it to become invisible, become immortal, change physically (from Dr. Jeckyll to Mr. Hyde) or mentally, or have made a deal with a devil to be something they are not (*Dorian Gray*, for instance), fits the bill.

If you can dream it up, you can use it. There will need to be a backstory and some logic to make the being believable though.

The most common creation is one that is part mechanical (sentient) or totally mechanical (*seemingly* sentient).

The Totally Mechanical Being

If entirely mechanical in make-up, then this type of being will run on sophisticated clockwork gears and probably need to be wound regularly. A mechanical being could also do a preprogrammed "job" using punch cards that direct the movements. The looms ran on similar systems to weave cloth and the data entry clerks of the 1960s and early 1970s created cards with holes specifying a code for computers of that era to read, so there are precedents, even if one isn't of 19th century creation. Cards like this riffle through the machinery in *The Difference Engine*.

A mechanical can be powered by clockwork, a small steam engine but also by a battery. The appearance of batteries much like the AA, C and D sizes we use today were in production by 1898 though the first models (possibly a bit larger and less dependable) were available in the late 1870s. At the turn of the century two manufacturers combined to create the Eveready battery company, thus a battery powered robotic worker could be very feasible historically as well as Steampunkably. Creating a new power source is also an option if it appears to have a feasible reason for working. It isn't just in *Doctor Who* episodes that human brains have been placed in mechanical men as power and guidance systems.

Be sure to make these creations Victorian though. That means the exterior could be etched with Spenserian swirls, engraved with flowers or vines or dragons or other mythic creatures. No surface was left empty of decoration and the genius who invents and builds these mechanical servants should follow suit.

Whether they are given a voice or not, mechanical soldiers will stand and move differently than the servant class of automaton. Servants might even be crafted to appear to be wearing skirts, mop hats, weskits and ties. Let whimsy lead your way.

The Partially Mechanical Being

If we take the bionic man as an example of the extreme augmented man and an amputee as a minor one, there is still a lot of opportunity for the mad or well-meaning scientist, mechanic, or mechanically minded doctor to turn a previously whole human (or animal) into something with enhanced abilities.

These are upgrades from wooden legs, hooks, and carved and belted on hands and feet. Those would be more historically correct, but we are creating a different world here. Whether the loss be from an injury that didn't respond to treatment, from an accident or a military action where amputation was necessary, the 19th century offers men and women in great numbers that would be of interest to our inventors. Although "ratting" is against the law, that never stopped anyone from putting dogs in pits with them to fight to the death, so perhaps the way characters get around the law (which was to protect dogs, not rats) is to set partially mechanical dogs among the rats (or totally mechanical ones).

The subjects receiving the upgrades will more likely be from the lower classes simply because it will be factory workers, men working the docks or ships, laying rail or digging in a mine, or former infantrymen who will be destitute and unable to find work because they are no longer whole. In England, London's East End and the manufacturing towns are places where henchmen can round up subjects for mad scientists. On the Continent, in the Americas, and other parts of the British Empire the cities will have similar areas in which to find the guinea pigs for the experiments, the folks who will receive the enhancements once they are perfected.

Steampunk stories where a clockwork heart replacement needed to be rewound in a sentient being have surfaced (George Mann's *The Executioner's Heart* for one).

In some cases, the reconstructed, perhaps reconfigured, beings will be affected by what they have endured. Some may be cowed and become extremely docile, but others will become vicious, perhaps even joyful in besting anyone who lacks their newfound strength or ability. They could be grateful to their creator or despise him or her.

The scientist/mechanic who builds these constructs must have a very good reason for the work done. If they are the villain of the story, then it is to gain power, wealth, influence in some way. If they are the main characters or related to the "good guys" side of the tale, then the goal will be to aid these misfortunates, even if in cases it is a misplaced belief that they are helping rather than creating "freaks" that the populace fears.

Depending on what augmentation is done, some of these "new" beings will require power sources and in other cases a simpler system can be used, for instance the key to wind a clockwork mechanism, which could be something they are capable of doing on their own.

Knowing what will be required of the partially mechanical being in the story before designing them would be convenient, but sometimes it is a brilliant flash of an idea that builds the being and lets the story follow what they are capable of and how they feel about their new state of being.

Thus, this is a case of deciding whether they are built for a diabolical purpose or are the result of an effort to help a person return to a more normal mode of existence.

The Restructured Biological

To create an animal capable of doing specific chores, mankind has been breeding beasts for centuries. Bigger draft animals for hauling large loads, smaller ponies with great stamina and sure-footedness on narrow mountain paths, better meat producers, better milk producers. The various breeds of dogs are an example of this for dachshunds were bred to go down holes dug by their prey, greyhounds were bred for speed, and various other breeds worked as four-footed infantry troops.

What the 19th century supplies us with is a *possible* way to combine features that normally aren't in a particular species' repertoire. In 1869 a Swiss scientist was working to identify what later was referred to as DNA, but it wasn't until the 1950s that research on DNA double-helix strands went into high gear. There still is a lot we don't know or haven't identified in regard to DNA. What was lacking historically was prior research and powerful enough microscopes. A thoughtful building of your Steampunk world can rectify those things. In fact, Scott Westerfeld has *his* Edwardian world the beneficiary of such a twist with animals being "built" for all sorts of specific functions, such as the whales that function as airships, complete with living quarters inside them (a la Jonah and the Whale).

Mark Hodder dreamed up dogs that deliver written messages and parakeets that repeat messages verbatim (with a few insults inserted) to the "addressee". He has giant swans that pull kites for solo aerial taxi service. These service animals are merely part of the Steampunk world his cast lives in. One of the mad scientists in the series had his brain placed in the body of an ape to out-jockey death.

Hodder has definitely taken the create-a-being idea between his teeth and shaken it like a terrier with a rat in the pit. While there is not a requirement at publishers to have an augmented or changed or specifically built biological being in a Steampunk tale, they have been appearing in the genre since the early Steampunk stories of the late 20th century.

Unlike with the Partially Mechanical beings, Restructured Biologicals usually have been bred – that is "born" – with the enhancements due to breeding of some sort. That's not to say that the "breeding" couldn't be done in a test tube. Or that, as noted in the Partially Mechanical section, mechanical legs or jaws or some other metal can't be added as well.

The Magically Created Being

There aren't as many of these creatures to deal with. For the most part they fall into two categories: those created via magic related to a religion and those created by an alchemist.

A homunculus is a small human, usually a man. The recipe to create this tiny being is to take human semen that has putrefied for 40 days in a container then inserted into the belly of a horse until it matures into a…well, a Thumbelina sized man (there don't appear to be any tiny females in the lore). The first alchemic recipe for the creation of a homunculus was written during the Renaissance. Homunculi frequently show up in fantasy and as Steampunk is a niche within fantasy, it wouldn't be farfetched to brew up a guy smaller than Barnum's Tom Thumb.

While alchemists tend to busy themselves attempting to turn base metal into gold or find the Elixir of Life, as Nicholas Flamel supposedly did, neither of these things has anything to do with creating a being. It may appear that because there are no magic words mentioned in the homunculi recipe that it doesn't equate to magic. However, anything alchemistically created was considered a form of magic during the Renaissance. Alchemy is considered to be a protoscience that lead to the development of modern chemistry and medicine, both elements that are part of both the 19th century and a Steampunk world.

A golem is another being built with a recipe, one that dates back to the creation of Adam in the Garden of Eden: take mud and shape it into the form of a man and breathe one of the secret names of God into it. A golem usually requires that last ingredient to be a written word inserted within it to animate the creature. To kill a golem, the slip of paper must be retrieved from inside it. Once that is done, the being becomes nothing but a lump of clay or mud. However, extracting it isn't easy. Any injury the golem receives is quickly "healed" as it simply reforms, shifting mud back into place. A golem can't speak and doesn't think for itself, but it takes orders from its creator religiously. But, as a golem is part of Jewish folklore, that's to be expected.

A Steampunk golem doesn't have to be constructed of mud or by a scientist or mechanic of Jewish decent or belief. It should have that bit of paper with a "magic" word inserted inside to animate it though.

For our purposes, the magic word could be whatever the person building it wishes it to be. Could be "Gloriana" or "Britannia" if they are in the employ of the Queen.

A mummy is another creation of magic. Once it was a person who was ensorcelled by an Egyptian (or Mayan or other ancient civilization) priest to guard the tomb of a king or queen or highly placed person – perhaps the priest's predecessor. It is inanimate, a dead man (or woman or perhaps an animal like a lion) wrapped in linen until the tomb is breeched by thieves. While 18th, 19th and 20th century archaeologists didn't consider themselves to be thieves, even though they were emptying the tomb, the ancient guard posted would "see" them as such. The mummy might be slow to act, particularly if thousands of years have passed, making it slow to wake, but it could act upon those ancient orders while the avid archaeological team is still on the site or not until the "spoils" have been brought back to one of the major western cities of Europe or America to be displayed and studied in the halls of a museum. But it will strike. And how do you "kill" a being created by ancient magic? Ah, that's for you to dream up! A mummy is a being created by magic, once human but no longer so.

The third type of magical being that can be related to religious fervor is a zombie. At least one type of zombie – the kind created by a Voodoo priest. These zombies can be the reanimated dead or merely a person so mesmerized and possibly affected by an infusion of snake venom to be entirely in the priest's control. Only a Voodoo master practitioner can create either type of zombie. He could do so at the request of a master villain, or he could be the villain himself. It's fairly doubtful that he'd be on the side of good after treating his adherents so badly. Zombies, even if still living humans, do not act on their own as normal sentient beings do. They are totally under the control of their creator's will.

The Paranormal Being

Zombies can fall under this category as well if created without the help of a friendly neighborhood Voodoo doctor. Cherie Priest turned most survivors of her desecrated Seattle into zombies by killing them through inhalation of a noxious gas leaking from the ground. These types of zombies can either kill with their bite or turn their victims into zombies as well.

George Mann uses zombie-like Revenants, which are a curse inadvertently brought back from India by returning soldiers who were bitten by people carrying the virus that causes this living death. The Revenants enjoy feasting on their fellow citizens and usually only are out at night when the fog in London allows them to snag prey easily. A few lucky sorts have recovered from the fever induced by a Revenant's bite, but not many. Fortunately, Mann's hero is one of the fortunate. Therefore, as opposed to Priest's zombies, Mann's Revenants are treated more like very dangerous victims of a plague, one more concentrated in the East End among the poor.

If you love zombies, find a new and possibly different way to create them, or give some of them leadership abilities so that they aren't all decomposing sheep. Whether they develop a taste for brains is up to you, but maybe you'd rather not perpetrate a cliché!

Thanks to Bram Stoker's *Dracula*, vampires are a logical addition to the Steampunk world. Like the zombies and Revenants noted in Priest and Mann, these are beings who were once human but turned into something different by a bite. Oh, they're still dead, but not decomposing like the zombies or Revenants.

Gail Carriger made her vampires part of the social set but also part of the vice of London. As fops, she plays them for comedic relief, but does swing back to them being very strong and powerful beings in her Steampunk world.

She also uses werewolves (the third type of being created by biting a human), segmenting them into the major part of the Victorian army and making their leader/Alpha her hero.

Using paranormals in a Steampunk tale turns it into a Victorian set urban fantasy, but to retain the Steampunkness be sure to add some fantastic machines!

Since I've been tossing together a possible idea here (not a terribly brilliant one but it should suffice for illustration purposes) with our scientist's journey to Mars, what the setup is still missing at this point is a created being. Rather than a biological, it makes sense to have a mechanical one who can act as an autopilot, do heavy lifting, and hopefully not need to use up any of the oxygen. It can remain a servant or be given a personality for comedic relief. What it does at this point is fill one of the requirements for a solid Steampunk setup.

Now in modeling the Steampunk stage, a bit more is necessary.

Victoria's World
1834 – 1901

There are specifics to consider working into your Steampunk world that will help your audience identify it easily. Many of them will seem self-evident but rather than have them slip from sight, we'll run through them in the following chapters.

In most cases these are tied to actual events or situations or organizations that are historically associated with Steampunk stories.

For instance, prior to 1860, the elements of the Industrial Revolution are far more mechanical than they are after that benchmark. After 1860 the Second Industrial Revolution kicks in with the emphasis on science and medicine. Some of the visibly moving machinery of the earlier era begins to disappear, replaced by smaller workings until the way things work begins to appear to be via magic rather than machine. When you consider the way a computer or the Internet or your cell phone or even television and radio works, isn't there an element that appears to be magic about it? Some consider that we still are in the Industrial Revolution, merely the much extended second leg of it.

Our late Victorian "invisible" workings belong to the telegraph, the telephone, to photography and moving pictures at the end of the era, to recordings of voices and music as phonographs arrive. Electricity is mysterious and then we move on in the Edwardian Era to those fantastic flying machines, the motorized ones – fixed wing manned aero planes and dirigibles, both with only propellers showing as moving elements. On the ground both diesel and electric powered motorized vehicles are spooking teams of horses hitched to carriages and wagons in the 1890s.

There is a quieter form of transportation as well – the bicycle becomes extremely popular in the late Victorian period.

Trains, of course, have visible working parts – the churning wheels, the men shoveling coal into the tender, even the steam streaming from the smokestack is a visible sign of something familiar at work powering the machine. The face full of cinders and soot that might greet anyone sticking their head out the window of a moving train is also a visual that can be used. At first the railways were used to haul coal and were powered by teams of horses. By 1830 the first Steam powered locomotive passenger service began on the Manchester and Liverpool Railway. Rail lines blossomed around the world in quick succession in the following years. Pick the country of your choice and just be sure research tells you it traveled to the destination you desire in the year your story takes place. Unless, of course, this is something you are altering for the sake of your tale. The earliest you can catch a train out of or into London historically is 1833 and the only place you can go to or travel from is Birmingham at that point.

The top speed of 40 miles per hour was reached in England in 1835, 78 mph (the record) in 1850, though 25 mph was the usual traveling speed, except through towns where it dropped by law (and for safety) to 2 to 4 mph.

Steel rails replaced the iron ones in 1857, at least in the real world, and there were different widths used by different companies which meant one couldn't necessarily use the other's line to reach a destination. In the "war" between the wide and narrow-gauge rails, Standard or narrow gauge sets the rails 4 foot 8 ½ inches apart and was first used by George Stephenson. His competitor Isambard Kingdom Brunel used wide gauge, a "broad gauge" of 7-foot $1/4$ inches. It took an act of Parliament to standardize rails to the narrow gauge, and by 1892 all railways complied in Britain. The U.S. and other countries had adopted the narrow gauge early on, the Baltimore and Ohio beginning to lay their rails in 1828. By the 1850s there were very few countries that didn't have a rail service of some sort.

In other words, trains are big business everywhere in the Victorian era around the world.

So part of the face of our Victorian world is based on the transportation and even what is visible in the workings of the machine, if not gears then pistons, whirling propellers on still-in-the-works flying machines, legs pumping away to propel a bicycle – and there are all sorts of interesting bicycles. Even some motorcycles bowing in in the 1890s.

The 1890s is also the decade that the first motorized automobiles make an appearance. They will be more in evidence from 1897 onwards.

In London people have been descending to the Underground train system since 1863. The first line only ran a few miles, but they were convenient miles. People were willing to put up with the soot from the steam locomotives pulling the carriages, so more tunnels followed, and the line expanded. Electric locomotives were in place by 1907, which means they are *historically* Edwardian. No reason why your characters can't have developed these earlier, naturally.

In 1834 the Palace of Westminster was mostly destroyed by fire. We know the palace better as the Houses of Parliament. The rebuilding of it in the current Neo-Gothic style began in 1840 and continued up to 1870. The most well-known feature is the Elizabeth Tower which houses "Big Ben" and was completed in 1858.

Balmoral Castle, at least the current one, began life in the 1850s. It had been a hunting lodge previously but after Victoria and Albert's first visit in 1848 things began to change. For one thing, the place was too small for a royal residence. Albert took a fancy to a corrugated iron cottage displayed at the Great Exhibition in 1851 and ordered the prefab to serve as the ballroom and dining room at Balmoral beginning in October of the same year. That sounds delightfully Steampunkish rather than historical, even though it is historical fact. Just asks to be tinkered with, doesn't it? Or used by some of your own characters. The rest of Balmoral went up between 1853 and 1856 then the older buildings, including the prefab iron cottage apparently, were demolished.

The bridges over the Thames are definitely a visual that can be used. Tower Bridge is the nearest crossing at the East End since the 19th century slums abut the Tower of London, but there was no Tower Bridge until 1894 (begun in 1886), which is when the bascule and suspension bridge opened. It needed to accommodate the tall-masted ships heading for the docks between the new bridge and London Bridge. The original mechanics to raise the bridge for a ship to pass were powered by pressurized water which was stored in hydraulic accumulators. The best late 19th century technology could supply. The bridge also featured gas lighting. Tower Bridge is the engineers' dream bridge of the era. At least in London.

The next bridge heading into the city is London Bridge, the site of a bridge since Roman times if not back to Neolithic ones. The British replaced a 600-year-old version prior to Victoria's ascension to the throne, opening it in 1832. Made of granite, it lasted until 1968. However, in 1896 it was widened by 13 feet. Edwardian surveys later showed that the bridge was sinking one inch every eight years. By 1924 (which takes us into the Dieselpunk era) the east side was three to four inches lower, but it wasn't replaced until the late 1960s.

Next bridge up the line from London Bridge is Blackfriars, built in 1769, repaired in 1833 and 1840 then replaced in 1869. Waterloo Bridge opened in 1817 but had a reputation as the bridge of choice for suicides in the 1840s. In 1841 an American wire walker died while attempting his act on this bridge. The Hungerford Bridge was first a railway conduit. Also called the Charing Cross Bridge, it opened in 1864. Today it is the site of a walking bridge near the London Eye. The Westminster Bridge was built in 1750 but replaced in 1862. It is currently the oldest bridge in use across the Thames in London. The Lambeth Bridge opened in 1860. The Vauxhall was the first iron bridge over the Thames and opened in 1809. It was replaced due to instability in 1816. By 1898 it had resisted efforts to stabilize the piers and a temporary walking bridge was built while the older one was demolished. The new bridge opened in 1906, well within the Edwardian period.

Beyond the Vauxhall is the Chelsea, opened in 1858, the Albert in 1873 and lastly the Battersea, built in 1799 and lit with oil lamps, then by gas in 1824 and after being replaced in 1890, no doubt had electric lights. Naturally, this doesn't mention any railway bridges that might have been built that didn't cross the Thames.

Most of London's bridges were toll bridges but one by one the tolls were dispersed with during Victoria's reign until in 1879 no tolls were in effect.

There is one Victorian route to travel from one side of the Thames to the other that doesn't involve crossing the water though. It goes beneath it.

The Wapping-to-Rotherhithe tunnel was built in 1843, the first modern tunnel beneath a river and the first beneath the Thames. Digging it cost the lives of ten men and £614,000 and when finished it was dank and alive with the constant sound of water pumps. Building it was a battle with quicksand and the Thames. The building of the tunnel is quite a tale but suffice to say that a project begun on the drawing board in 1798 at last opened in 1843, the final successful venture taking fifteen years to build. By 1870 when the Tower Subway tunnel dove beneath the river, the engineer in charge of the project took the elements that the Brunels (father and son) had used on the Wapping-to-Rotherhithe dig and evolved them. For those who might have a need for tunneling equipment in their Steampunk story, reading up on the Victorian inventiveness that burrowed beneath the Thames is well worth the time. The disasters encountered could even supply ideas for events in the tale.

There were other rivers running through London. Some were integrated into the canal system in the 18th century, such as the Lea. Others were so polluted they were covered over and became unofficial and then official sewers. The Fleet is the most well-known of these, but similar destinies belong to the Walbrook, the Wandle, the Tyburn, the Effra, and the Westbourne. Stamford Brook was covered over in 1900, probably the last to have such an indignity visited on it. The Westbourne had fed the man-made waterway, The Serpentine, in Hyde Park in the 1730s, but the Westbourne was polluted by 1834 and flowed only below ground by the 1850s.

Talking about pollution brings us to one of the most recognizable elements of London, particularly in the Victorian era: The London Particular, the fog. Consisting of sulfur dioxide (a poisonous gas) and soot from fireplaces and industry's furnaces, it has been described as blackish, yellowish, and greenish. Thick enough to blanket the light of gas lamps on the streets, it was cloying and caused respiratory problems to those living inside its insidious confines. London has always had fogs, the situation of the River Thames and swamp land making it a natural extension. The Industrial Age took the evil smelling soup of earlier ages and soured it further. But the fog gives Victorian London some of its flavor. All sorts of atrocities can occur in such blackout conditions – and did. Jack the Ripper is merely the best-known villain to benefit from the Particular's blanketing effect.

One of the things contributing to the Particular, of course, are the steam engines that chug in on the rails from locations throughout the island kingdom. The London Bridge station opened in 1836, Euston in 1837, Fenchurch in 1841, Vauxhall and Waterloo in 1848, King's Cross in 1852, Paddington in 1854, Victoria in 1862, Charing Cross in 1864, Moorgate in 1865, Cannon Street in 1866, St. Pancras in 1868, Waterloo East in 1869, Liverpool Street in 1874, Blackfriars in 1886, and Old Street in Islington in 1901. It's easy to see why the Particular was as thick a pea soup as it was in Dickens' and Doyle's tales.

Breathing in London was even worse in 1858, the year honored by the moniker The Great Stink, and that was coming off the extremely polluted Thames. It was also the source of regular cholera plagues. Charles Booth's Poverty Map of London (1889) clearly shows how closely the wealthy and the poor lived to each other. Fortunately, it and other maps of London and the countryside (the Victorian Ordinance Maps) can help a Steampunk writer pinpoint locales and correctly name features of the landscape. In the case of Booth's map, it helps place factories or lodgings for characters in the correct parts of town. A major sewer project was launched in 1859 to correct things but the improvement to the water was an inadvertent improvement once the improved sewer system was in place. No reason why your characters can't make the condition of the water their priority though. The sewer system did something to the face of London that we accept as part of the landscape today – it contributed to the building of The Embankment. The Chelsea Embankment was built in 1854 but it was the major section of the Thames Embankment that housed part of the new sewer system in 1862.

An element that holds promise for those interested in building a more elite Steampunk world is the Great Victorian Way. It was proposed and given the okay – Prince Albert himself gave it the thumbs up – in 1855. Unfortunately, the need for the sewer project after the Great Stink in 1858, sucked funds away before it was off the drawing boards. If built it would have been a ten-mile loop around what we'll call the better parts of London and would have featured a glass roof over the street, railways, shops and houses. The architect responsible for the marvelous glass building that housed the Great Exhibition in 1851 was the mastermind behind a part of Victorian London that never came to be.

Railroads weren't the first things to bring Industrial Age progress to London. The Grand Junction Canal opened in 1801 and the first section to be linked to it in the Capital was the Regent's Canal in 1816. When the London and Birmingham Railway arrived, business on the canal increased because coal for the steam engines was being shipped on the barges.

The Regent's Canal Dock opened in 1820, though it was later known as the Limehouse Basin. The area became home to communities of Chinese, as did Shadwell. Tea wasn't the only thing being shipped in from the Orient though, opium was also inbound, and during the late Victorian period Limehouse hosted a number of opium dens. The use of drugs was not illegal, merely frowned upon as a weakness much like over indulgence in alcoholic spirits or visits to the numerous bordellos and "molly" houses (which catered to homosexual tastes – homosexuality being a jailing offence through most of the period).

The pub visited by the men of Scotland Yard while still headquartered in Westminster was The Rising Sun on Great Scotland Yard.

Which allows us to segue into the coppers. Whether it's the constable on the street or an undercover bloke from the Special Branch, the police are a very distinctive element in Victorian London if for no other reason than there had never been as large a uniformed policing unit in place prior to this.

According to Charles Dickens, Jr., in his *The Dickens Dictionary*, the Metropolitan Police (the official name of the force then and now) used this setup: "Within a reasonable distance of nearly every house in a populous district there is, besides the local police-station, a fixed police point, at which a constable may always be found from 9 a.m. to 1 a.m. If the constable at the fixed point be called away on special duty, his place is taken by the first patrol who arrives at the vacant place." Handy to know? For an authentic Victorian look and feel, most definitely. Doesn't mean these constables need to be fully human, does it?

GEARED UP WRITING STEAMPUNK

The final element that rounds out a Victorian setting is where one goes for entertainment. It was, after all, during the later years of the Victorian period that Gilbert and Sullivan reinvented musical theatre with their popular light operas. Of course, the music halls where variety acts reigned hadn't been replaced by the movies yet. Besides comedy skits and song and dance numbers, there were likely to be acrobats, magicians/illusionists, escape artists (like Houdini) or hypnotists. There were no standup comedians yet – they are part of the future.

Higher brow performances were given in the better theatres. For instance, Her Majesty's Theatre in Haymarket was the center of ballet in London in 1843. Shakespeare continued to hold sway but there were other playwrights as well. Frequently one didn't go to see the play but the *player* as Henry Irving and Ellen Terry pulled them in for the Bard's work at the Lyceum (managed by Bram Stoker) in the late Victorian. Built in the 18th century, the Lyceum Theatre reopened its doors in 1834 on Wellington Street, having needed to shift a bit when the street was created. It was further improved in 1882 and in 1884 the circle fronts were altered and redecorated. Along the Strand was the real hot spot for late Victorian theatres. The Tivoli Music Hall was located there in 1890 at 65-70 ½ and had a capacity of 1,510. The Adelphi Theatre was across from it.

The Old Vic had opened as the Royal Coburg Theatre in 1818 but became the Victoria Theatre in 1833. It was located opposite Bridge Road in Lambeth. The Lyric was built on Shaftesbury Avenue in 1888. Its stage door was on Great Windmill Street, its façade that of the house that preceded it at the location, built in 1766. The Savoy Theatre opened in 1881 facing the Embankment.

For a location that sticks around throughout the period, there is the 17th century Mogul Tavern in Drury Lane. Altered in 1847 it was renamed the Mogul Saloon. It became the Middlesex Music Hall in 1851 with a change of venue. Remodeling and additions were accomplished in 1868, 1872, 1875 and 1892. The Oxford Music Hall opened in 1861 at 6 Oxford Street but burned and was rebuilt in 1869, then redone once more in 1892-93. This time it had entrances on both Tottenham Court Road *and* Oxford Street. And these are just a handful of places your characters might visit and leave whistling a new tune.

One can also visit the Great Exhibition in 1851 and see the Crystal Palace built to house it – Prince Albert was very involved in gathering the wonders of the Industrial world under one roof. Other exhibitions would follow in London, but not at this location. The Crystal Palace is moved to Sydenham Hill and additions were made beginning in 1852 and numerous events from a Handel festival to a cat show were held there.

Visit the zoo in Regent's Park – it opened to the public in 1826 and added the Reptile House in 1849, the Aquarium in 1853 and the Insect House in 1881. The British Museum dates to 1759, housed in Montague House in Bloomsbury (current address specifies this on Great Russell Street). In the 19th century there were many additions made, most accomplished by the purchase and demolition of 69 houses on adjacent properties to add additional wings. The Rosetta Stone had been acquired in 1802 and the Elgin Marbles in 1816. In 1822 the Library swelled with the acquisition of George III's vast library, which wasn't entirely accessible to the public until 1857, though it was opened for special visits during the Great Exhibition. In the 1840s and 1850s the Museum sponsored overseas excavations which resulted in its large collection of Assyrian items.

If your story requires the military, British soldiers are being shipped hither and yon. The British East India Company in India had its own military force backed up by the "Queen's Men", military regulars. They were involved in the three Anglo-Afghan wars and figure in such historic events as the Retreat from Kabul in 1842, also known as the Massacre of Elphinstone's Army, and the Mutiny of 1857. With the creation of the Raj in 1858, after the Mutiny, the East India Company was no longer in charge – the military and politicians sent from London were. It may be worth noting that the Great Indian Peninsular Railway and the East Indian Railway both began laying rails in 1853-1854 and that it was possible to cross Northern India from Allahabad to Kanpur in 1859.

The Crimean War of 1853-1856 is best known for the disastrous Charge of the Light Brigade, part of the Battle of Balaclava in 1854. The British fleet did a bit of watery dueling with the Russian Black Sea

Fleet as part of the Crimean conflict, too. Might they have had some Steampunk enhanced weapons? Well, if they had, perhaps the results of the war would have been different, too.

In the mid to late Victorian period what the various empires in Europe had their eyes on was Africa though. What conflicts erupted between the British and a foe usually involved the people who already lived there. Such as the Zulus, remembered in many minds for the impossible standoff between the vast Zulu army (3,000 to 4,000 men armed mostly with spears) and a small detachment of British soldiers (150) at Rorke's Drift in January 1879. The Zulu chief honored his brave remaining opponents by withdrawing his troops...at least that's the way it ran in the movie version (*Zulu*). Whatever his reasons were, the Zulus did melt away.

The British tried to annex the Transvaal area from the Dutch (South African Republic or Orange Freestate, aka Boers) in 1877 but only grumbling appears to have been the result then. By 1880-1881, the Boers were armed and determined to keep the British out. It was a short war, but the South African Republic won the round. Could be they had called in some nifty Steampunk gear? Well, at least in a tale you might hatch that uses this setting, it could happen, right? Wars make such lovely opportunities for inventors and megalomaniacs.

Diamonds bring out the greed, and it was diamonds that were first discovered in 1869 on the banks of the Vaal River. The first was 47.69 carats, a white diamond that would become known as The Star of South Africa, but also as The Dudley Diamond. The first four diamonds mines went into production in 1871, the largest one was known locally as The Big Hole, but the owners preferred to call it The Kimberley Diamond Mine.

And if diamonds don't give your characters a lust, perhaps gold will, for there was gold discovered at various South African locations in 1840, 1870, 1873, 1881, 1882, but the largest find was in 1886 with the Witwatersrand Gold Rush. In fact, this find is part of the Golden Arc, an area that stretches from Johannesburg (a city that owes its birth to the gold rush) to Welkom. This wasn't exactly British soil, was it? The Boers farmed the Transvaal area as well as did British landowners. A few shoulders were bumped too hard and in 1880-1881 a series of engagements between the two fractions broke out during a ten-week period. It wasn't so much a war as an armed conflict between neighbors. Then along came that big Witwatersrand gold rush. As the mine was British owned but on Orange Freestate land – Boer land – it wasn't long until words – and probably fists in some quarters – were being thrown. The result was a raid in 1885-1886 which lead over the next decade to the outbreak of the Second Boer War in 1899. It lasted into 1902 and this time it was the British, using both regular troop forces and guerrilla warfare techniques, who stomped the opposition. And "stomped" fits since not only were huge numbers of troops sent out but a "scorched earth" policy and internment camps for the captured lent to a very dystopian set up – even among the victors who were plagued by disease as well as combat duties.

Where there is a war in the making, there is a market for a Steampunk entrepreneurial character to step in and let the tale unfold, whether entirely or partially. It may not be played out on the Isle of Britain, but it is still part of Victoria's Empire.

But speaking of that Isle – there are other cities to consider using that are on the British homeland. Manchester's leap to the big time began in 1780 when the first cotton mill was opened there. The Industrial Revolution sent it surging into the minds of merchants during the Victorian era. It was even known as Cottonopolis and Warehouse City. As the most productive cotton center in the nation – by 1853 there were 108 cotton mills there – workers flocked to the city for jobs in the mills. Of course, that can lead to trouble, and it did – the Peterloo Massacre of 1819 when troops were sent against workers demanding voting rights. The Luddites were also active in this area between 1811 and 1817, rioting and demonstrating against the modernized power looms and spinning frames in the factories that left the cottage industry textile workers with no customers. Wages were incredibly low to begin with. This all happened in the pre-Victorian era but it was part of Manchester's rise to fame. Manchester was the site of the first railway station and didn't officially become a city until 1853. It is notable as being host to socialism, the Labour Party, and women's suffrage during the second half of the century, and the Manchester Ship Canal that stretched to connect to the Mersey, a tidal river, in 1894. Excellent dystopian setting, even if they do have a few telephones in 1878.

Liverpool is another Industrial Era boom town. Rather than factories, it is shipping of merchandise from Manchester that does it well. It and Manchester are the first two cities to ever be linked by a railroad in 1830.

Go a bit further north and you'll hit Glasgow, the city that beat out Edinburgh in population figures in 1821. The city even beat out Sir Robert Peel and had the first municipal police force in the world up and running in 1800. Otherwise, they were involved in nearly every sort of business available from leather processing to textiles, furniture making, carpet manufacturing, pottery, printing, and even the manufacturing of cigarettes in the later Victorian period. By the close of the century Glasgow was known as the Second City in the Empire. For an inventor searching for a place that is hungry for new products, he (or she) might do well North of Hadrian's Wall.

Victoria's England has much more to offer but these highlights of the visual 19th century offer distinctive flavor. The East End London or possibly Manchester slums, the fog, the trains and other modes of transport, the now very visible presence of the police force, the pestilence, where to go for music or for hallucinogenics, the new buildings, bridges, and...well, the whole cloth of Victoria's Britain and the outposts of the Empire lay at your command. Leave a large part of it untouched, but tweak away at other elements as required.

Edward's World
1901 - 1919

While the 1890s already possessed a number of things that would be associated with the early 20th century, it was still solidly the Victorian era because Victoria herself didn't follow the Bard's stage direction and "shuffle off this mortal coil" until 1901. Edward had been waiting a long time for his turn on the throne. Victoria's era covers over sixty-five years, but the Edwardian is allotted less than twenty. Still Edward did leave his mark, although he died in the middle of the Edwardian Era. Odd but true. Blame the discrepancy on historians.

Not only was Edward "Europe's Uncle", he'd been a good will ambassador for his mother's empire, touring the world and making friends. And influencing the way gentlemen dressed.

Laws had been passed to make some things pleasanter for some of his subjects. The sewers and cleaner drinking water had done a lot to improve Londoners' health, though there was a new threat to the air: gasoline powered motor vehicles were beginning to turn up in vaster quantities. There are still a lot of horse drawn vehicles, plenty of trains and the rails beneath the city in the Underground were branching out further and further. Those who could afford to do so were availing themselves of the expanded transportation system by living further out of town in suburbs and traveling into the city via rail.

The music halls are still doing a nice business, but as the film industry begins to gather steam, the end of the Edwardian era will find some stage shows giving way to moving pictures – silent ones, naturally, unless you have a tinkerer determined to add sound earlier than it appeared historically, which was in *The Jazz Singer* in 1927.

Speaking of historical things, the Zeppelin makes its official appearance, but so do bi-wing planes, in the early years of Edward's reign. Many inventors had been working on them but in 1903 the Wright Brothers of the U.S. managed the first motorized manned flight though they returned to their shop to tweak things and apply for a patent. When it came through in 1909, Wilbur Wright headed for Europe to interest prospective customers in placing orders – which they did. In Paris Wright set off an inadvertent fad as the cap he wore was in even greater demand than the plane. Well, it was cheaper and didn't need to be housed in a separate building.

The Edwardian Era features races between owners of the various newfangled devices – both automobiles and aero planes. The races were run from one city to another or with flights across the English Channel most frequently. Mechanics were always in demand, and men with new ideas welcomed in every barn – garages and hangers not being the norm yet.

It is the era in which department stores begin to be more in evidence, though they had begun to exist in the later decades of the 19th century. Names like Harrods, which opened its current Knightsbridge store in 1905, and Selfridges, which opened on Oxford Street in 1907, are where Edwardian Steampunk heroines might shop. Selfridges was changing the way things were done – the goal to make shopping a pleasure not merely a necessity. Fortnum and Mason was still the supplier for specialty foods as it had been since opening in 1707 in St. James Market. Fortnum and Mason took an extraordinary step in 1914 though – it promised that any employee who joined the Army at the outbreak of war would have a job waiting for them when they returned at its close. It was an unheard-of offer at the time.

J.M Barrie wrote *Peter Pan* during this era and P.G. Wodehouse's writing career first took flight in it as well. Newspaper editorial cartoons pictured Shakespeare quaking before marquees featuring plays by W. Somerset Maugham. George Bernard Shaw had been doing well in the late Victorian, and his plays continued to fill seats in the theatres. Noel Coward was a child actor appearing on many stages, one of his parts was as a Lost Boy in the play version of *Peter Pan*. When a new edifice was planned it wasn't in the Art Nouveau style popular on the Continent but in a style that harkened back to Christopher Wren and was termed Edwardian Baroque.

The first trans-Atlantic wireless signals were transmitted, and typewriters were now being mass produced. Vacuum cleaners, fire extinguishers, diesel locomotives, stainless steel, tear gas, SONAR, and refrigerators all make their initial bows. In science radium is discovered, Einstein comes up with the new theory of relativity/gravity, quantum theory is being tossed about in physics circles and there is chatter about genetic heredity, atomic structure and superconductivity as well. And during the Great War, the hemlines on women's skirts begin to raise, and while the boys come home, the hemlines remain above the ankle. The future is galloping in on both steam and diesel-powered hooves.

London hosts the Olympics the summer of 1908.

The Savoy Theatre builds a hotel next door in 1903. Some upgrading occurred at the theatre as well for it was the first theatre to light the auditorium with electricity rather than gas, though there was gas lighting installed for use if the electricity failed.

The first international passenger air service began in 1919 between London and Paris, the plane leaving Hounslow Heath, not far from today's Heathrow Airport. Don't confuse it with the sort of schedules we have today though. Airplanes were still small and limited in the number of passengers. Think of civilian passenger flights as agreements between anyone with a two-seater plane and someone willing to pay for the gasoline, ground fees and flight time. It won't be until the 1930s that planes large enough to hold more passengers are built and the zeppelins had a good handle on that market by the late 1920s. Historically, that is. There are several Steampunk tales that have created civilian air service similar to that of trains though most often with dirigibles rather than fixed wing planes. Airships *are* one of the visible elements of Steampunk but only because history has been altered to move their development and expansive use of earlier than it occurred.

Luxury steam liners had become popular in the later Victorian but the name that rings through the time period for most of us is that of the White Star Line's RMS *Titanic*. The *Titanic*, of course, hit an iceberg in the Atlantic while on its maiden voyage en route to New York. The date was April 14, 1912 with the ship slipping beneath the waves entirely on the 15th. Of the 2,224 passengers and crew aboard over 1,500 were lost, most of them 3rd class passengers and men because of the "women and children first" rule enforced by some of the officers in charge of loading the life boats, of which there was an insufficient supply based on the number of people aboard. Oddly enough, the only group of passengers to not suffer any casualties were the children of Second Class. One of the reasons given for the disaster was that the steering on the *Titantic* was of a new design and some features were the exact opposite of those that the crew was familiar with. Ah, technology raises its head once more for us to tamper with if so wished.

The *Titanic* wasn't the only major sea disaster of the Edwardian Era though for there was a great loss of life on May 1, 1915 when, while on its 202nd voyage, en route from New York, the RMS *Lusitania* was torpedoed by a German U-boat (submarine) when 14 miles off the coast of Ireland. The ship was gone within 18 minutes. Of the 1,959 aboard, 1,198 died. There were two explosions though the Germans swore they fired only one torpedo. The second is thought to have been ammunition covertly stored beneath decks, but someone with a Steampunk frame of mind can certainly dream up another reason. All characters in Steampunk novels don't hail from English speaking countries, after all, and there was a war on at the time.

The first decade of the Edwardian also sees a clash of forces previously undreamt of: the Suffragettes vs the Metropolitan Police.

There were two distinct groups representing the suffrage for women movement in Britain: the National Union of Women's Suffrage Societies and the Women's Social and Political Union.

The National Union was under the auspices of Millicent Fawcett. Formed by molding a few smaller organizations into one in 1897, it advocated peaceful methods to urge a changing of the laws. Members organized meetings, distributed leaflets and urged the signing of petitions. This was too tame for Emmeline Pankhurst and the women of the Women's Social and Political Union, formed in 1903, who believed in militant and radical means to get attention for the cause. Mrs. Pankhurst's followers were the women chaining themselves to railings, causing destruction to businesses and setting fire to the mail. This was frequently seen as illustrating that women were too emotional and unable to control themselves to be given the vote. They did get the headlines though.

Headlines weren't necessarily what they wanted and arrests for their civil disobedience followed. Within little more than a dozen years, 1,000 women were jailed for offenses related to the cause. In

1909 those imprisoned began to go on hunger strikes. The government ordered them to be force fed, a painful process that involved being strapped down and a tube inserted in their mouth or nose. It didn't deter the women, though the health of many suffered.

Of particular Steampunk use is the creation in 1913 of The Bodyguard within Pankhurst's organization. The women so assigned were to protect Pankhurst and other executive members, frequently with violent behavior. A Bodyguard seems a perfect position for a created being to hold.

The outbreak of war in 1914 changed everything. Many of the women turned to their families' needs, and the ranks of suffragettes shrank. In Pankhurst's group there was a split as only a few remained militant while others looked for less violent ways to urge the change in laws. At the close of the war in 1918 the Representation of the People Act made it possible for women to become elected members of Parliament but full suffrage only came in 1928 in Britain, which means it lagged behind other parts of the Empire for New Zealand had been letting women vote in all elections for quite a long time by then.

Of further interest may be the fact that green, white, and violet were the colors adopted by the W.S.P.U., and they frequently showed up in fashion, represented by the use of amethysts, pearls and peridots in jewelry. Work the colors into the wardrobe of any British female Steampunk character with mechanical interests and abilities.

Remember that the second part of the Boer War leaks over into the Edwardian, so if you're looking for a change of scene, heading for the Transvaal in Africa is a consideration until around 1910 when things wind down.

The Edwardian era is split by two things. One is World War I, which Britain was engaged in from 1914 to the signing of the Armistice in 1919. The second is that Edward himself died in 1910 and his son George became king. We don't change the name of the era it's simply that George V had to deal with the War to End All Wars (which, unfortunately, it didn't do).

If machines running on steam and diesel on the ground and in the air don't mark the period, then the face of the war most definitely did. While trench warfare had been used in conflicts during the 19th century, they hadn't been the "face" of warfare yet. Now they were.

Poisonous gas warfare was also an important element, for canisters tossed or fired into the trenches killed men in great numbers or put them out of action.

Motorized ambulances (frequently driven by women who also knew how to service or fix their "flivvers") were in use and the legendary aerial dogfights between dashing pilots in bi-wing planes frequently lead to spectacular crashes.

Nineteenth century Britain had had 4% more women than men in the late Victorian years and had considered that a serious social problem. When the young men went to war, nearly an entire generation was hobbled. Two-thirds of the deaths were battle related which was a drastic change from casualties in the wars fought during the 19th century where disease was the main cause of death. There were over 37 million military and civilian casualties (dead and wounded), of which 10 million were military deaths and over 7 million civilian deaths. Britain alone had nearly 890,000 soldiers killed and after the release of men held in Axis prisoner-of-war camps, there were still over 100,000 men missing in action.

These figures can supply us with many wounded personnel that a Steampunk genius/maniac could use to build a new army, or replacements for later in the war when men were in short supply. But it can also give us those missing people who might surface later not quite as human as those with replacement parts.

During the war women take on many jobs that were previously held by men. Some of them could be interested in engineering, have worked with fathers, uncles, brothers, sweethearts, if not becoming engineers through schooling prior to this. After the war, young women wed much older men simply because the war decimated the supply of men in their age group as well as sent many home either physically or mentally wounded or both.

In 1917, King George officially changed the royal family name to Windsor to divorce them from their strongly German heritage (not only had George I been a Hanoverian when he became king after the death of Stuart Queen Anne, but George V's grandfather Albert had been from the German states).

And as the world finally takes a deep breath in 1919 as the nations put pen to the Armistice, the creative forces that were fired up at the thought of a new century and new opportunities settle behind drawing boards and begin work on new schematics.

It does appear that the things that mark the opening decade of the Edwardian era are powered by gasoline engines far more than steam ones – those horseless buggies and flying machines – and that the years after Edward's death when George V ruled were marked by major losses of life – the *Titanic, Lusitania* and World War I itself. From high spirits to catastrophes, that's the Edwardian Era in a teacup. We'll leave the British here and back up a few decades, change continents and head west now, pardner.

Weird West
U.S., Canada, Australia, New Zealand, Tasmania
1870 – 1890

The world of Weird West Steampunk gives us a landscape and characters far removed from those of London. But it also narrows our scope – for the most part, Weird West tales are set *after* the American Civil War and in the Gilded Age (1870s-1880s), although there is no rule that says an earlier niche in western history (or colonial development) can't be used. Regarding America, the halt might be called at this point because the U.S. Census Bureau announced that the frontier was closed in 1890. There were now enough people living west of the Mississippi to no longer have any large tracks of land that weren't broken by settlement. Oddly enough, western expansion with homesteading was just getting started at this time in Canada, aided by improved transportation and the expiration of land leasing rights to ranchers. However, even in Australia, New Zealand and Tasmania, things are falling into the same rhythm in the 1870s and 1880s.

We're focusing more on these decades for two reasons: 1) that prior to the 1870s there hadn't been much technology based transportation into the outlands in any of these countries and 2) once 1890 arrives the 20th century is steaming down fast on nearly all areas of the globe. Still, we're going to fudge a bit when an opportunity that shouts for Steampunk attention comes to light.

Because the United States, Canada, Australia, New Zealand and Tasmania all had things in common, they each match the requirements for a Weird West sort of tale.

Consider:

- Each have wide open spaces

- Each have native tribes (aboriginals) who clash with settlers

- Each have European arrivals living in rough conditions

- Each have men (and some women) who wear, and use, weapons

- Transportation is still in the process of materializing with rails for train tracks being laid, and frequently laid by immigrant workers from various nations

- All three areas have gold rushes from the mid-19th century onward, with some having silver as well

- Each have cattle and/or sheep ranching in common

- The towns that are built tend to have saloons before they have churches

- The camps that come before the towns tend to have a population that is nearly all male and nearly all males under thirty years of age

- The first women in the area, if they aren't wives and daughters dragged along, will be prostitutes (although in New Zealand and Tasmania the mining community grabs the local native women rather than do without)

- Lawlessness is frequent because order is maintained by military forces expected to cover large distances with minimal men

- Vigilante committees fill the gap – justice is swiftly dealt with "necktie parties", or hunting parties retaliating against aboriginals

- Dystopian situations can be the norm because living conditions are harsh and dangerous

Rather than look at each of the countries separately, we'll consider the opportunities history gives us in categories.

Territory

If you are sticking with the U.S., the territory is anywhere west of New Orleans, north along the western side of the Mississippi so Missouri, Kansas, Nebraska, Wisconsin, then west along the Canadian border into the Dakota, Montana, Idaho and Washington areas then south along the coast down to the Mexican border and on back to the Mississippi. All places within this loop are your playgrounds. This is the physical territory most often covered by Weird West tales.

Canada has a slightly different look when it comes to the great outdoors for it lacks the deserts of America, though perhaps it is merely a case of substituting the icy north for them instead. Although it is owned by the U.S., the Alaskan Territory (it doesn't become a state until the mid-20th century) really belongs in the same category here. For simplicity's sake, we'll say anything west of Toronto and Quebec and North of the U.S.-Canadian border is open for Weird West Canadian Steampunk expansion.

Australia definitely has desert areas, but it also has mountains and a heck of a lot of beaches since it is an island continent. Melbourne and Sydney should be reserved for our Weird Urban territory, but the rest of the continent is open game for more Wild West style Steampunk tales.

New Zealand is a long thin curve of broken island (it is in two pieces) southeast of Australia, and Tasmania is a spot of land off the southern coast of Australia, probably once part of the continent that broke free. There are also hundreds of small islands included in the territory which might work if you are looking for a hideout for a mad scientist to develop evil machines or perform unspeakable mutations on...well, on living things. Some areas have rain forests, if that is of interest.

And should you be straddling a decision about what year to place a story, it might be convenient to know that transportation of criminals to Australia was discontinued in 1868. In 1855 Van Diemen's Land officially became Tasmania. Van Diemenslandt was the name the Dutch had given it in honor of the head of the Dutch East India Company who sent Abel Tasman off on a voyage of discovery in 1642. The 19th century British colony residing there asked to have the name changed.

One continent, two larger islands and hundreds of smaller islands make up the area of these colonial lands in the Southern Hemisphere, but a lot of the same things are happening in this region as they are in the vast open lands and mountain ranges of North America.

The majority of Steampunk stories that have American settings take place during the 1870s and 1880s which just happen to be the main decades of the Indian wars, particularly on the Plains. However, we're really not limited to two decades. When it comes to backstory, you should consider reading up on what was going on prior to these years in the event it could be altered to create the world for your story. Some of these elements will be the discovery of all gold and silver veins prior to 1870 (and there are a number of them), the formation of the Republic of Texas and subsequent entry into the union in the 1840s, the entire American Civil War, and the expansion of the railways from one side of the continent to another, a venture that was completed in America in 1869.

Natives and Agencies of the Law

After the Civil War the U.S. military shifted gears. There were forts established along the various wagon routes west (the Oregon Trail and the Santa Fe Trail, to name just two) earlier, but most troops had been withdrawn to the eastern theatres of war in the early 1860s. When the war was behind them, the nation had a well-trained and staffed military force that had to go somewhere. Under General Phil Sheridan's guidance, it went west to police the natives. Apparently, Sheridan's feelings were that the only good Indian was a dead Indian…or one that had been beaten into submission and confined on a reservation. Not a forward-thinking fellow was Phil.

More and more settlers were pouring west and were interested in things on Indian land. Didn't matter if it was reservation land or not if it looked good to them, which is why the Indians got shortchanged on a lot of deals.

Interestingly enough there was one clan of the Comanche that had avoided contact with any Europeans so well that no one knew they even existed until 1871. That's when the trouble began with the Quanhadi lead by chief Quanah Parker. His clan had wealth in horses and cattle and since they'd been invisible previously, peace treaties had never been signed with them. As more and more Americans and European immigrants pushed west, the Quanhadi were invisible no more. The 4th Cavalry took the field against them but rather than engage in open battle the troops destroyed these Comanche's camps, cattle and horses, stripping them of the means of survival. Chief Quanah Parker surrendered the summer of 1875 with barely 1,500 of his original 5,000 people left to move onto the reservation.

The Red River War of 1874 was a series of campaign clashes with the Comanche (some of them being the Quanhadi), Kiowa, Southern Cheyenne, and Arapaho. The tribes' wandering days were over, the military decided. They needed to be off the Great Plains and tucked away on reservations in Indian Territory (modern Oklahoma). Oddly enough, the reason the tribes were on the move was that they were in search of buffalo. The herds that had once been vast were pitifully small now, a result of expeditions of American buffalo hunters taking advantage of the demand for buffalo hides (a result of a new tanning process developed in 1870). Decimating the herds was like bulldozing the natives' shopping mall since buffalo provided meat and the materials for tools, tents, and other supplies. The various nations aligned themselves as a combined front against the military when it arrived, believing (sadly as other tribes in the east had in earlier years) the prophesy of a medicine man that if they joined forces they would be immune to bullets and best the Americans. It was a short war and we all know which side got shortchanged.

That's what was happening around the Texas Panhandle, but in Arizona Territory the Chiricahua War with Cochise dragged on from the 1860s to 1873. The Yavapai and Western Apache were attempting to hold their own from 1871 to 1875 but were forced onto the San Carlos Reservation in the end. Chief Victorio and a band of renegade warriors broke off the reservation in 1879 and began a guerrilla war through Apacheria that crossed the border and involved Mexican authorities as well. When Victorio was killed by the Mexicans in 1881 his followers joined Geronimo, who managed to continue the war against settlers, miners, and the military into 1886 when he was forced to surrender and was transported to a reservation in Florida to keep him far from his homeland.

The Black Hawk War of 1865 to 1872 resulted when sixteen clans of Ute, Paiute, Apache and Navajo attempted to stop further Mormon settlement in their lands. It took military intervention in 1872 to halt the deprivations of the combined tribes under Ute Chief Black Hawk's leadership, though Black Hawk himself had died of tuberculosis in 1870. Just a thought, but what if a Steampunk scientist emerged from one of the tribes who managed to keep Black Hawk's body moving and guiding his people in those years before the military stepped in to bring the conflict between the tribes and the Mormons to a halt?

Probably the best known of the Indian Wars is the Great Sioux War of 1876-1877 as this was a result of gold being discovered in the Black Hills of Dakota Territory, which were sacred to the Lakota Sioux and Northern Cheyenne tribes. This is the war in which Custer made his "last stand" in the Powder River country in 1876.

Looking for a different part of the country? Consider the Modoc War of 1872-1873 in Northern California and Oregon. It was the final Indian war to take place in the Pacific coast states and was photographed (still scenes, of course, though perhaps your characters have already invented moving pictures). Considering that when the groups met to talk peace a military man was murdered, think what a money maker a film that included that would be! Remember, convicted murderers were still hung in those days, though whether the Modoc who pulled the trigger was ever sent to trial is debatable.

The Nez Perce War was very short, June to November in 1877. It resulted from the decision to shift the Nez Perce from their traditional hunting grounds in Oregon to a reservation in Idaho, though the trail lead into Montana as well. In fact, the tribesmen fought the military along a retreat line of 1,170 miles that brought them forty miles shy of the Canadian border before they surrendered.

The Bannock War is another conflict that lasted only a few months in 1878 in southern Idaho. The Crow War or Uprising or Rebellion was even shorter when warriors broke off the reservation in Montana and were corralled back on to it by the military in September 1887. The tribes who had once roamed the plains and mountains and deserts of the American West had been bested by a well-armed and well-trained professional army, with only a few attempts at freedom yet to come, but they will come outside of the years that make up the Gilded Age. As far as the government was concerned, the frontier was closed, existed no more, by 1890.

In the military the Steampunk author has opportunities to upgrade weapons and even the types of soldiers if some mechanical or mechanical enhanced ones appeal to you. Let's not leave out the soldiers of the other side of this coin though – the warriors. Enough tribesmen had been educated to give us the opportunity to have a young brave show some mechanical genius when sent away to school by a broadminded charity type. What if this now educated and brilliant individual brings some "toys" to the battlefields? What if it was mechanical warriors and some whiz-bang newfangled weapons that Sitting Bull had at his disposal when he ran into the long knives along the Little Big Horn River in 1876? What if it was a case of something that grandstanding George A. Custer brought to the field that inadvertently caused the massacre that followed? Maybe it was the result of industrial espionage or insufficient testing or lack of replacement parts available for this new technical "advantage" before the battle that was the problem??

Let's look at this another way yet. What if that shaman who claimed the tribes would win out over the long knives (sword wielding cavalry) if they joined forces was right? What if once the dust cleared it was the settlers who were being herded onto reservations or into prisoner of war-like camps by the braves? It either leads to a reverse of the dystopian life the tribes lived on the reservations or to a massive headache for the chiefs involved as they loaded the captives onto boats bound for the eastern bank of the Mississippi.

Steampunk opens all doors for characters, frequently slamming them shut in the face of *real* history.

Oddly enough the North West Canadian Mounted Police were formed to protect the Indians, particularly from whiskey peddlers and settlers who pointed rifles and pistols at the Indians then pulled the trigger. Formation of the group dates back to 1873 and was the brainstorm of a British Army officer, Lt. W. F. Butler, who wore out a lot of boot leather (and horse shoes, no doubt) doing a trek of 1,000 miles across Canada in 1870. Upon his return he recommended the creation of a mounted force that was well equipped to deal with policing the North West. A few years later the North West Mounted Police came into being with the signing of an Act of Parliament back in London. That first force consisted of less than 300 men, 22 of them officers. The youngest recruit was sixteen. They had more horses than they did constables, sub-constables, and sergeant majors.

The original force headed off, in 1874, on an 800-mile trip toward the Canadian Rockies (northern section of the Rocky Mountains) to do their duty. It wasn't a happy trip. Short of firewood and water, and dealing with plagues of insects, most of the horses died and the equipment they'd been issued turned out to be totally inadequate for the job. Prairie winds destroyed tents and the original uniforms did little to protect the men from the elements. Then a guide found them and led them to a camp (called Camp Whoop-up, in modern day Alberta) which the American whiskey traders ran. When the Americans heard the Canadians were coming, they evacuated the premises and the fort was taken without a single shot fired.

The N.W.M.P. set up base at Fort Macleod south of Calgary that year and spread out the next year adding Fort Saskatchewan, Fort Calgary and Fort Walsh. Duties expanded out on the frontier for once the Canadian Pacific Railway (begun in 1874, finished in 1885) worked its way westward, so did further settlers. As a result, Mounties were delivering mail, doing record keeping for births, deaths, and weather endured, the last making them a source of information for incoming farmers. They also "fought prairie grass fires and helped starving and destitute immigrants." Fortunately, their uniform changed to the distinctive, and more duty ready, Red Serge that consisted of the red all-weather coat, riding britches and boots, Stetson with wide flat brim, belt, weapons and white lanyard.

Although termed "police", the North West Mounted Police were called in to assist in a military position during the North West

Rebellion and the Battle of Duck Lake (Saskatchewan) saw them suffering heavy losses in 1885.

Although it is beyond the years we're dealing with, it's worth mentioning that when gold was discovered in the Yukon in 1898, it was the Mounties job to keep the peace and to check the boats (over 7,000 of them!) before the eager miners tumbled in for the journey up the Yukon River to Dawson City. The duties far overwhelmed the available men and recruitment posters went up quickly.

To be Mountie material in 1898 and applicant had to be between 22 and 40 years old, be "active, able-bodied...of thoroughly sound constitution" plus they needed to produce "certificates of exemplary character and sobriety." They had to know their way around horses and ride well. Joining the Force had a man signing five years of his life to the service, but he received free "rations" and "a free kit" upon joining. I'm taking the "kit" to be uniform, saddle, weapons, etc. to outfit him out for duty.

While the phrase "the Mounties always get their man" could be considered a cliché, it does appear true that "Canada is the only country in the world where the police are heroes."

But even so, they could do with some Steampunk equipment or created beings (or need to go up against some created beings).

Time to jump on a ship and head to the Southern Hemisphere to another land that caters well to Weird West tales because it has much in common with events in western North America.

If you look at the treatment of the Australian Aborigines by the incoming British from 1790 on through the 1920s it is quite easy to be appalled. They were treated not like people who needed to be chased from a spot of land a settler fancied but like vermin.

The Australian frontier wars began when Europeans arrived back in 1788 and didn't really end until 1934. Queensland was the most populated area with a third of the indigenous peoples living within its territory. Which means it saw the bulk of the conflicts between native and European immigrant, though historically the majority of those first immigrants weren't there of their own choosing.

Other than the settlements that grew to become cities, Europeans were spread out in small groups at stations (ranches or farmsteads) and conflict with the natives arose only when resources were stretched for either group. American Indians and the people of New Zealand acquired weapons like those of their European neighbors, but the Aboriginals of Australia seem to have stuck to the spears and other weapons used in hunting or against their enemies traditionally. This put them at a disadvantage, particularly after 1850 when technology provided the European troops, police and settlers with Colt six-shot revolvers, Snider breech-loading single shot rifles then Martini-Henry rifles and the rapid-fire Winchester rifle. Against advanced weaponry, the Aboriginals stood little chance of winning out.

The list of engagements in the first half of the century is varied and shows forts being opened and then closed, and officials giving settlers the okay to shoot as many Aboriginals as they wished. It saved the troops the trouble of dealing with them, no doubt. The larger confrontations always came when Europeans swarmed into a particular area though, such as in 1892 when the Wangkathaa took exception to the arrival of gold seekers in the Coolgardie area in Western Australia.

In the Northern Territory the war between the local natives and the incoming Europeans began in the 1860s and saw regular skirmishes through the years, the final ones just as vicious as the earlier ones.

It is easy to see a criminal mastermind rounding up Aboriginals with even more dazzling Steampunk weaponry and forcing them to bow to his will. Mix in some beaten former convict or soldier captured and tossed in with them and a once dystopian situation might be redeemed with the hero and his fellow prisoners constructing something from pilfered parts to strike back. It also allows shaman magic to have a part in the proceedings.

Just off the south shore of Australia is Tasmania, or as it was known in earlier years, Van Diemen's Land. The natives, the Parlevar, here had been cut off from their cousins on the main continent since the end of the ice age but were 5,000 to 10,000 strong when the first British prison ships arrived in 1803. They've been called the "simplest people on Earth" because unlike the natives of Australia proper, the Parlevar never shared in the technological advances made by their cousins. To us these will seem very primitive but boomerangs, hooks, sewing, bone tools of all kinds, barbed spears, and maybe even the ability to start a fire from scratch never made it across the water barrier between the two land masses. Their lifestyle was a migratory one based on the seasons for they lived off the land. Through contact with Europeans their population was whittled to only four full blooded Tasmanian natives left in the 1860s. The Parlevar language had been entirely lost by the late Victorian era. Most of the decimation of natives is the result of their having no resistance to diseases from outside their own community. In some cases, it took only two days to wipe out entire communities with disease. It didn't help that the military was given Royal Proclamations to post boundaries for the Parlevar and even declared martial law against them. Natives without passes allowing them to cross settled districts were fair game for settlers interested in making a fast pound or so for a bounty of £5 was offered for an adult and even children were worth £2 when brought in.

Even if bounties weren't paid on dead Aboriginals, there was money to be made on any of their skeletal remains (though full skeletons and skulls were the real prizes) from the 1860s on as scientists were rabid to study them anthropologically, which is why this information was included here. Historically, there were extremely rabid scientists interested in the Parlevar tribesmen and women. As a group of people cut off from the rest of the world for so long, they were of paleoanthropological interest. One poor woman, Truganini, was even exhumed in 1878 (she'd died in 1876) and her skeleton hung on display until 1947 in the Tasmanian Museum. The most gruesome disrespect for a native happened in 1869 when William Lanne's skull and scrotum were removed shortly after his death, the latter turned into a tobacco pouch.

As horrific as that is, a really nasty Steampunk villain could do this to someone who was his rival or make it a habit to present such "gifts" to men he wishes to test for lack of humanity.

Further to the east are the islands that comprise New Zealand where the Māori were in sympathy with the natives in the American West...or would have been if they knew they existed. While conflict between settlers and the Māori resembled all-out war as early as

1845, the majority of the confrontations were in the 1860s on up to 1872. As happened to the indigenous people everywhere, when European immigrants took a hankering to a piece of land it simply didn't matter to them that it was home to others already.

British forces in New Zealand were not only larger numerically, they were carrying technologically superior weaponry, the Pattern 1853 Enfield for the troops and the Calisher and Terry carbine, which was a shorter rifle, rested against the shoulder of a Forest Ranger. Only officers and the rangers carried revolvers with the military favoring the Beaumont Adams, a five-shot .44, and the bush fighters the single action of the Colt Navy .36 1851 Model. The rangers of Von Tempsky's second company of bush fighters also carried Bowie knives.

The Regulars' campaigns were more military engagements while the 65 men of the Forest Rangers (formed in 1863) carried on bush warfare using guerrilla tactics. Losses were high on both sides but statistically less for the British who put 18,000 men in the field against 4,000 Māori warriors during the Taranaki and Waikato campaigns in the 1860s. British losses were 800, or close to 4.5%; Māori, 1,800 or 45%.

As with the engagements between military or civilian forces in North America and Australia, there are mechanical opportunities for Steampunk inventors for either offensive or defensive war machines, and for either side if a forward-thinking native utilizes such services. Scientists tampering with viruses or developing chemicals for use in war are viable Steampunk directions. But if you put a different spin on the history, it could be the side that won historically who can be the loser. After all, once someone acquaints a native with the appearance of a substance lusted after by Europeans, they could buy nearly any Steampunk genius. There are, you know, gold in them thar hills.

The Miners

One of the things that drew men, women, and children away from civilization in the American East was the gleaming promise of gold or silver in their future, in their pockets, in the West. And as the mining camps boomed, so did the demand for goods shipped from the East. And if business is booming, it's an excellent opportunity for inventors to improve on methods of extraction, isn't it? Extraction of precious metals from ore and extraction of precious coin from men's pockets.

The first women to make it to the mining camps were usually prostitutes and a few long suffering wives who, when their husbands died as a result of illness or gunfight or deadly accident, had to find a way to make their own way. Not all these ladies acquired a new husband within hours of the other's demise, although many did. Others went into business for themselves – and not necessarily the mattress trade. No, they used what they knew best – cooking in most cases – and set a high price on their goods. But by the Gilded Age improved transportation changed the face of mining simply because people could get where they were going much faster than they had back in the mining rushes in California, Nevada, Idaho, and Colorado.

It was grueling work to be the first man on a claim in the 1870s though so any mechanical device or steam or clockwork minion that could make life easier would be welcome. Of course, there were other things that caused trouble. Gambling halls, poor liquor, and an insufficient supply of women "manning" the cots and beds, were quickly in place to trim the pockets of the miners. More amusing ways to entertain and clean out wallets can be found by Steampunk characters, be it with mechanical toys, biological experiments or humans enhanced with mechanical parts – all are logical in a Steampunk universe. But so are ways to ensure that those manning the gambling tables extracted more gold from pockets than any miner dug up in a lifetime.

In the 1870s our miners will be headed to unearth "Custer's Gold" during the rush in the Black Hills of South Dakota and Wyoming in 1874 (the peak being 1876 and 1877), and the Bodie rush in California of 1876-1880. Gold is discovered in what is now White Oaks, New Mexico in 1879. The 1880s are quiet were gold is concerned but it's in the spotlight once more with the Cripple Creek rush in Colorado in 1890, the Mount Baker rush in Washington state beginning in 1897 and continuing into the 20th century, and the Nome rush in Alaska in 1898. A little out of the Gilded Age but still viable.

For silver, the 1870s feature a new silver strike in Virginia City, Nevada (The Big Bonanza of 1873), plus finds in Leadville (Oro City in 1874), Aspen, and Gilman districts in Colorado, Globe, Tombstone

(1879), and the Bradshaw Mountains in Arizona. The Silver Bar Mine was discovered by a soldier on patrol in New Mexico's Mogollon Mountains in 1870. In 1883 Silver Creek Canyon, also in the Mogollons, was supplying silver. The 1890s have the Cripple Creek (1890) in the Creede District in Colorado and Cochise County in Arizona.

It was copper that began being pulled out of Cleopatra Hill that gave birth to Jerome in Arizona in 1883, a find that continued to be worked until the price of copper fell in 1884, but it was copper that was being mined in Bisbee, Arizona Territory in 1877, too.

What do all mining rushes have in common? Populations that are nearly all male, and often fellas in their twenties. Gambling. Drinking. Weapons being carried and used, not always expertly. Prostitution. And these camps either "grew up" to be settled communities when the wives and families and churches began to move in or faded to just footnotes on old maps.

It isn't just the U.S. that is rich in precious minerals though. There are gold strikes in British Columbia, just north of the U.S.-Canadian border, with the Cassiar rush in the 1870s, plus the Cayoosh and the Tulameen rushes both in the 1880s. Then, in the 1890s, the location shifts to the Klondike in the Yukon.

In the 1880s British Columbia sees silver finds at Nelson, then, in the 1890s, in Slocan, Kaslo and New Denver.

Gold drew men to the Australian continent from 1851 through the middle of the 1890s. As we're sticking with the same years as the Gilded Era, we have the Palmer River rush in the 1870s in Queensland, and the Westralia in the 1890s in Kalgoorlie, Western Australia.

Still, it was the earlier gold finds that sent the Australian European population soaring, taking it from nearly 438,000 in 1851 to over 1.1 million in the early 1860s. To differentiate the new arrivals from earlier settlers, the incoming immigrants were known as "new chums". Whether the term continues being used later. . . well, that's up to your characters. Some of the old timers would certainly still be using it.

Tasmania's first gold find was in 1847 in the Brandy Creek area (renamed Beaconsfield in 1879. There were numerous small finds through the years, enough to draw Chinese miners to the area. But it was in 1877 that the big strike came. A gold reef was found on the sunrise facing slope of Cabbage Tree Hill, the find going down in the history books as the very profitable Tasmanian Reef mining area, which is, oddly enough, located near Beaconsfield. Within two years underground mining had begun with three shafts sunk, one of which was worked until 1914.

Iron ore deposits were unearthed along the Savage River in 1877, but were judged too low a quality ore, and only revisited later in the 20th century. That doesn't mean your Steampunk characters wouldn't find it worth their while far earlier...or that you can't alter the original find to a better quality of ore.

Copper mining also belongs to the Tasmanian landscape though it shifts the miners to the west coast of the island and begins in 1893, lasting a full century before being abandoned.

There is a very Steampunk sort of name given to a section east of Mount Owen, which is in the West Coast Range of Western Tasmania. It's called Philosopher's Ridge and was the spot most miners in the area called home beginning with the Iron Blow, the first major mining on the mountain in 1883.

Not long after gold made headlines in Australia, it turned up in Coromandel, New Zealand, in 1852. There were rushes in the 1860s, and then the 1870s rush followed in Kumara and Dillmanstown.

From 1879 on into the early 20th century there is a shift to something that is still in demand: coal. Extracting it is a dangerous business and there are accidents in the mines. Thirty-four miners were lost when candles caused an underground explosion at the Kaitangata mine in 1879, but in 1896 sixty-five miners died from inhaling poisonous gases or the explosion that followed at the Brunner mine in 1896. This could be worked as either a dystopian sort of existence or an opportunity for a Steampunk inventor to correct the problem...or run into competition that doesn't want him (or her) to succeed.

If mining resources in New Zealand stirs the Steampunk pot of ideas you have stewing, the two parts of the island yield not only gold and coal, but silver, limestone and iron ore to tempt characters, too.

Railroads

Do you know the difference between rail*roads* and rail*ways*? It's the country they are being built by. The British call theirs "ways" and the American's call theirs "roads". Big difference, huh? Well, it was. Why? Because British railways frequently traveled alongside already familiar paths, often pathways or canals that had been built to ship goods along only a few years earlier – on the island of Britain, that is. In the United States the trails became the roads as they traveled where no wagon or stagecoach traveled in many places. Even though the railways laid in British Empire lands often weren't following established trade routes the same as they did "back home", they were still called "railways" though. Just another example of Americans coming up with slightly different terms of elements shared in common by both countries. As we've been visiting the Wild West before going off to similar set ups elsewhere in the world, let's concentrate on the U.S. first again.

Prior to the Civil War, most rails were laid in the Northeast because that was where the manufacturing centers were located – New England. The South was still mostly under cultivation as was most of the country west of the Eastern seaboard. Settlement was still scarce the further one pushed West and got skimpier the further you went. Yes, there were settlements on the west side of the Mississippi, but very few had anything remotely like train service or, if they did, booming train service. There was that very wide Mississippi River in the way of rail progress and bridges needed to be built. All of this came after the war and was linked to the cattle business rather than westward expansion.

Cattle began being driven north out of Texas after the Civil War. The era of the cattle drive is 1866 to 1886 when millions of head traveled along the Chisholm Trail, the Goodnight, and others, headed for the nearest railhead. That's when the railroads really began pushing west. The destinations were in Kansas first and the names of the towns read like a list of western movie locations to us today:

Abilene, Dodge City, Wichita, then on to Cheyenne in Wyoming Territory. Cattle were also driven further west to various forts but we're talking about the rails, so forget about those unless that suits your setting preference.

The earliest herds were largely wild cattle, but cattle ranches were soon the norm and kept cowboys and vaqueros busy most of the year. Extra staff was hired on (drifters) to fill the quota needed for a cattle drive and they were paid upon reaching the destination after the cattle were sold to buyers ready to ship them to the slaughter houses in Chicago.

The railroads *and* the cattle business offer Steampunk options not only with machines but perhaps breeding a new type of walking beef. The trail did wear the cattle down. It was a long walk and sometimes a long stretch between watering holes. A cross between a cow and a camel, perhaps? The railroads can be given stronger locomotives or special cattle cars as well. If the train is carrying any ore shipments as well, the security could be enhanced up by your handy dandy Steampunk inventor/mechanic. And the towns themselves might need to be altered to make them even more of a mecca for dusty, lonely cowhands fresh off the trail. Of course, if trouble breaks out, local law enforcement could be where you do your tweaking. A lawman with a reputation who was injured and got a mechanical hand or arm to replace the one he was famous for fast draws with is possible. There is a short Steampunk story in which the local sheriff was an Abraham Lincoln automaton who ended up out of a job after Lincoln was assassinated and fellas who drew against him always lost because while they could fill him with holes, he didn't go down and had the opportunity to take them out once their guns were empty.

Cherie Priest has a locomotive with heavy duty alternations in its schematic in her second book, though it appears to merely be firepower that is the core of the renovation. We could create a mechanical arm to lift cattle from the feed lot into the cattle car or create a refrigerated car long before they were available. Not for cattle, but for shipping all the oysters that seem to have been on the menu of every restaurant and saloon on either side of the Rocky Mountains. Or invent entertainment cars as well as upscale dining cars to bracket those Pullman cars after 1865 – or a really swanky sleeping car prior to the arrival of Pullman's if using a setting prior to the 1870s.

The first transcontinental railway in the States (and territories as there were a lot of landscape that hadn't been granted "state" status yet) was completed in 1869 with rails that headed out of San Francisco meeting up with those coming from the east. They met in Provo, Utah. There are several smaller railroads already active and if a town wanted to really get on the map now, it needed to have a train depot and regular traffic on the rails coming through. When it got passed over in favor of Cheyenne for the Union Pacific line, Denver had a heck of a fund-raising committee working to build its own rails to connect with the mainline. They weren't alone. Virginia City, Nevada, had the Virginia and Truckee Railroad hauling ore and passengers from the heights of Mount Davidson, down mountain to Carson City then on to Reno for connections with the Central Pacific. Railroads will be one of the first things any prosperous mining town will have on their Christmas lists. In 1877 the mine owners in Deadwood in the Black Hills were stuck running gold to the rails in Cheyenne on the local stage line until rails got punched through to them fifteen years later, which was passed their golden heyday. They'd probably appreciate some Steampunk assistance in dealing with the landscape involved much earlier – it wasn't exactly ideal for laying rails.

The Southern Pacific route didn't begin consolidating plans to run through the lower tier of states until the 1870s. Like the Union Pacific/Central Pacific link up, San Francisco was the starting point – or end of the line, depending on which direction a passenger began their trip from. The rails reached Bakersfield, California in 1874, but the first locomotive didn't make a run between Los Angeles and San Francisco until 1876. It was crossing the river at Yuma, Arizona Territory in 1877. By 1880 the first train had arrived in Tucson. The tracks were running way ahead of regular locomotive service for the rails reached El Paso, Texas in 1881, just beating out the Atchison, Topeka, and Santa Fe there. By then traveling from one coast to the other on a collection of railroads through the southern states was much easier. Unlike the northern line, the southern one went in for advertising that linked their name with travel for pleasure and in 1898 created *Sunset* magazine to further that image.

If you have a character traveling along the Atchison, Topeka, and Santa Fe Line from the 1878s into the 1920s, they might find the train stopping at a station that features one of Fred Harvey's restaurants where pert young waitresses will be happy to take their order for a quick meal during one of the train's stops for water. There are dining cars on other railroads but not on the AT&SF which contracted Harvey for the chain of restaurants. What your Steampunk characters choose to alter or keep the same here is entirely up to you. Seems a shame not to do *some* tinkering though, doesn't it? Maybe put some coin operated automats in for passengers not traveling first class? Have automatons as waiters or manning the kitchen?

In the event you weren't aware of this, it is the railroads that instigate the formation of different time zones in the United States. Prior to November 1883, they were dealing with 300 different local times which made the creation of timetables a real headache.

If you're looking for a specific railroad line or wondering whether there was one in a section of the country where you'd like to build your Steampunk world one, the Library of Congress has a collection of railroad maps dated 1828 through 1900 in their online section of aids for teachers.

Now when it comes to the rails in Canada, there are rails laid in the eastern providences early on. The Champlain and St. Lawrence Railroad was the first rail line in 1836, but it isn't until the Grand Trunk Railway project is complete that Canada has steamed toward the future. Although the rails were in the provinces of Ontario and Quebec for the most part, the Grand Trunk had the honor of being the longest railway in the world in 1867. The Victoria Bridge was built to accommodate it and was opened by Edward, Prince of Wales in 1860. The bridge itself was a wonder of the era for it was tubular in construction and spanned the St. Lawrence River. That is definitely something to catch the eye of a Steampunk engineer – of course, they'd put it all together in a slightly different manner but just as successfully.

GEARED UP WRITING STEAMPUNK

In 1876 the Intercolonial Railway linked Nova Scotia and New Brunswick to the Grand Trunk in Quebec. Profit-wise, it didn't work out as well as hoped, but the Canadian Pacific Railway, which was completed in 1885 more than met all expectations. Running from St. John, New Brunswick, to Vancouver, British Columbia, it was the final link from the Atlantic coast to the Pacific Coast and was instrumental in helping Vancouver become a major shipping port. While these aren't the only railways built in Canada, they are the ones characters might hop on or off of in a story – or cause one to grind their teeth, or plot to stop or stop construction on.

In the Southern Hemisphere, New South Wales has the honor of being home to the first rail service in Australia. It wasn't a passenger line but carried coal in 1831. By the close of the 1880s, the Main Southern, Main, Northern, and Main Western lines were making travel far easier for the locals. Of interest for an engineer might be the building of the Woy Woy Tunnel and the first Hawkesbury River rail bridge.

Melbourne in Victoria had a first in 1854 with the Melbourne and Suburban Railway. Expansions in rail service in 1862 to the gold diggings in both Bendigo and Ballarat expedited mining needs.

The first line in Queensland opened in 1865. Western Australia had to wait until 1879, but Southern Australia had steam locomotives on rails in the 1850s. Railway travel was ever increasing throughout the closing decades of the 19th century.

Rail lines in Tasmania were freight lines rather than passenger ones. The first opened in 1871, another four during the 1880s, and two in the 1890s. What was being shipped to the ports for export were ore: copper, iron, zinc, and tin. Timber was one of the major exports in the 1880s.

Over in New Zealand, major engineering projects were needed before rail service was up and running. In the 1860s the first major project was underway: the Lyttleton Tunnel which necessitated drilling through volcanic rock. To ship coal to port in the 1870s track needed to be run through the northern lands held by the Māori tribe. Bridges over gorges, a viaduct and the spectacular Raurimu spiral switchback stretch of track laid in 1898 to create a more navigable gradient are some of the engineering projects that might interest a Steampunk engineer. If he (or she) is looking for a challenge, the various projects connected to the railways in New Zealand would probably be mouth wateringly tempting.

Another way to utilize the railroads is to create better ones. Faster ones, stronger ones able to pull longer batches of cars.

What you do with Steampunk is make improvements – sensible ones and creative ones – for things that did exist in the period.

If your characters are interested in machines, that is. They might be interested in hooved beasts, though.

Sheep and Cattle Barons

One of the iconic pictures of the Old West is of mounted cowboys trailing cattle across wide sweeps of countryside. Steampunkers can use this as well, so let's look at when everything got started and when the drives went into decline.

The real drives of wild Texas longhorns didn't begin until after the Civil War. That's when the railroads began inching into the western lands and new military posts were opening. Both offered markets for beef.

So, the drives began in 1866 and continued into the 1880s. There were 1,500 to 3,000 head (that's 1,500 to 3,000 *cows* – although that's a generic term to a cowboy since there were a lot of steers), and to keep them from losing too much weight during the months on the trail a good day was a meager twenty-five miles traveled. Still cattle fell prey to disease and lack of fodder and water in some stretches. Once they reached the railhead a buyer was on hand to bargain with the trail boss. Money exchanged hands, the cowboys (regular ranch employees and drifters hired on specifically for the drive, usually ten to fifteen in number) were paid and proceeded to spend their wages at the saloons and bordellos of the cow town before drifting on or heading back to their home ranch.

The same happened regarding drives to the forts since there was usually a nearby town that catered to the soldiers' needs for relaxation through drink, cards, and female company.

One of the famous cattle trails that headed from Texas to the railroad cow towns in Kansas and Wyoming Territory was The

Chisholm Trail that met the rails in Abilene, the first of the cow towns in 1866. Fort Worth prospered from the drives as well, offering a place to rest and restock supplies, but it wasn't on the rails itself until 1876. By 1871 the Chisholm was rarely used as the railroad had punched further west, making it to Dodge City, but it saw a second life in the 1880s when the Atchison, Topeka and the Santa Fe rails reached Caldwell, Kansas, and made the route viable again for a while. The Goodnight Trail serviced forts further west prior to the arrival of the rails in the west Texas and eastern New Mexico Territory. Cows that boarded the trains were headed for the slaughterhouses in Chicago.

The Montana Territory cattle companies didn't fare as well as those in Texas. But the first herd of Texas longhorns was brought in in 1866. Running cattle on the open range here wasn't as profitable. As the mining camps tapped out, ranchers managed to hold on. But only until the combined drought of 1886 and harsh winter of 1887 (known as The Winter of Death) killed off large numbers of cattle. Ranching continued but not on the same scale in the north.

The American cattle drives were killed off not by lack of demand for beef but by homesteaders moving in and erecting fences out of that newfangled stuff, barbed wire, to keep the cattle off their property. One of the things they really got ticked off about was that the Texas cattle were bringing in a type of flea or tick that caused disease among the domestic stock.

That's what got farmers worked up in those parts. Over in New Mexico it was the idea of sheep farmers moving into cattle country that got men drawing iron on each other, declaring county scale wars and hiring on gun hands as well as livestock hands. In fact, if the fellows tending the livestock couldn't shoot worth a darn, chances are they wouldn't have a job long...and even more likely that they'd be pushing up daisies in a landscape that didn't cotton to daisies in the first place.

The Lincoln County War (New Mexico Territory) of 1878 is an example of this...a bloody example. One of the participants hired on as a gun was a fellow known more familiarly as Billy the Kid.

Sometimes it didn't even take sheep in the equation to rile things up. The Johnson Country war along the Powder River was just cattle men at each other's throats and the U.S. Cavalry was sent in to settle things in the end in 1892.

What can we do with this Steampunk-wise? Well, part of Steampunk deals with biological experimentation. Instead of sheep, perhaps it's a new breed of ...well, something different than mutton or a combination of mutton and pork...portton? Let's go back to that nasty Texas tick/flea that brought disease along with it. A terrorist organization might have dreamed up some new biological terror to unleash. Maybe they are the descendants of Spanish dons who not only want back the land deeded over to the U.S. at the close of the Mexican War in the 1840s, but all the territory west of the Mississippi, including that above the line in Canada? On the cattle drives the chuck wagons could become dirigibles complete with sleeping quarters for the cowboys not on sentry duty. Would certainly save a fella from having an unwelcome insect or snake join him under his blanket at night.

In the same book that she had the well-armed locomotive, Cherie Priest rewrote Texas history so that it never joins the Union but remains a separate Republic and promotes the use of oil considering how much of it is gushing out of the ground in their territory (although historically, the oil industry in Texas booms in the 20th century, from the 1930s onward). What if you have a similar situation only have the mining states banding together to form their own Republic to profit more from the ore being mined? You could tie it to the effort to move the U.S. from the gold standard to the silver standard, something that Nevada and Arizona could certainly get behind considering how much silver was dug up within their borders. Of course, you'll have to go back and make sure that Nevada doesn't manage to gain statehood in 1864 in time to vote Lincoln into a second term. That could be easily accomplished considering that the State Constitution had to reach Washington D.C. by a specific date and it wasn't finalized until the only way to meet the deadline was to put it all in one really long and expensive telegram – and that's real history. If the lines went down somewhere along the way thanks to tampering (and a really big, created being tearing through them) Nevadans would have missed their chance.

Cattle moved into the Canadian west in sync with the Mounties. In fact, the first cattle "town" in Canada is Fort Macleod. The first small herds were brought in from Montana in the 1870s, and all ranches were located near Mountie stations at first. British Columbia, the foothills of the Rocky Mountains, southeast Alberta and southwest Saskatchewan were where the large herds were chowing down on Dominion lands (i.e. government lands). Ranchers leased the land rather than own it. Once the Canadian Pacific Railway was built in the early 1880s, transportation to get beef to market allowed ranchers to up their income and the size of herds. However, by 1892 most of their land leases were up and settlers (referred to as "sodbusters" by the cattlemen) were petitioning the government to open the country to homesteading, something that had been going on south of the Canadian border in the U.S. for decades already. The large ranches argued against it, naturally, and seemed to be winning the legislation battle until new elections put homestead friendly men in office. That meant the ranches switched to advocating auctioning of water rights in 1896, hoping to cut homesteaders off at the well. A devious Steampunk tinkering villain or hero could devise some clever way to halt the opposition in its boots.

The terminology changes when we saddle up Down Under for the Outback is where the "stations" (aka ranches) are located, and these large tracks are overseen by a "grazier" rather than a rancher. Cowboys are "jackaroos" and a roundup is a "muster". Should you have a heroine saddling up to ride herd, she'll be a "jillaroo".

The original cattle brought into Australia were all English breeds: Hereford, Angus, and Shorthorn. The climate and landscape were hard on them and they were later replaced by Brahma, but that will take a while. Cattle ranches were more prominent from the 1880s on, most of the large herds established by 1915. The largest cattle drive was 20,000 head lead by Nat "Bluey" Buchanan. He and his jackaroos took them from Queensland to the Northwest Territory, though there were trail losses due to ticks, disease, and dry terrain along the way.

Over in New Zealand the first Angus cattle arrive in 1863, imported from Australia, which means there were smaller stations earlier than the 1880s. This shipment was of three bulls and four cows. By 1883 there were Shorthorns at the stations. Far more of the stations appear to be in Southland, the lower of the two islands.

Now if we talk sheep, that's really where the action is when it comes to livestock in Australia and New Zealand. The sheep stations in Australia are usually found in the southeast or southwest sections of the continent. In New Zealand they are in the high country of the south island. The same terminology applies to sheep men, though they can also be termed "pastoralist" or, if unwelcome, a "squatter". Gathering the sheep is still a muster.

The first sheep arrived in Australia in 1788 and were barely a handful compared to the numbers that would follow. By 1820 there were 100,000 sheep, by 1830 there were a million, and in New South Wales in 1840 there were four million that swelled to thirteen million by 1850. Therefore, we can say there are a heck of a lot of sheep in Australia by the 1870s. In New Zealand the Walter Peak Station was operational in 1860 near Lake Wakatipu on the south island. Fortunately for 21st century writers, Lady Mary Anne Barker wrote two books about her life on a New Zealand sheep station during the 1860s. Chances are that things won't change much over the next few decades, so it should be a helpful guide for a writer looking for a station at which to plunk down a Steampunk story.

Both cattle and sheep lend themselves nicely to the biological mutations created in Steampunk labs. Then again, a rival might come up with a tick delivered disease to wipe out his competition's herd while giving his own animals the antidote. As a reference or idea generator, historically it wasn't until 1897 that hoof and mouth disease, which can be contracted by any cloven hooved beast, was identified as a virus.

One last animal to mention and this one is a four-legged predator rather than two legged cash flow. It's the *thylacine*, also known as the Tasmanian tiger or Tasmanian wolf. Because it preyed on domestic livestock, settlers hunted it to extinction – last one seen in the wild was killed by a farmer in 1930. It had striped hindquarters, a snout that appeared more canine than feline, and species-wise was a carnivorial marsupial. The thylacine is included because it appears to be the result of tinkering in a Steampunk biologist's lab although it was from Mother Nature's. It can certainly be reconfigured or retrained by a Steampunk villain interested in clearing the neighborhood of pesky neighbors, or to keep people under his dystopian thumb. Decimating their flocks or herds with a thylacine pack or pride would certainly discourage them.

Outlaws

There can be all kinds of outlaws cluttering up things in the Old Steampunk West. They can have really nasty firepower. They can be part cyborg or totally mechanical beings run amok or specifically created to do exactly what they are doing – robbing stage coaches, trains, banks, express shipments, mining operation or Army payrolls – or shooting it out with anyone they are sent after.

You can use real life outlaws and rearrange their lives, augment them mentally or physically or bionically, or turn them into total lab creations that look awfully realistic. Perhaps they burn alcohol as a fuel source and can guzzle bad whiskey faster than the local drunk can down it.

Outlaws also rustle cattle, take on jobs as temporary lawmen, or work for the megalomaniac who wants to take over this neck of the plains, mountain, or desert.

Outlaws could *be* the law in a dystopian Old West where folks are forced to work in the mines or in the back or upstairs bedrooms of the local saloon and bawdy house. One of the outlaws could be the boss.

The American West's most wanted, and thus most remembered names, frequently fed out of the Confederate Raiders, the Missouri branches being the most famous among them. Cole Younger and his cousin Frank James were riding with William Quantrill's raiders, causing havoc among pro-Union/anti-slave Kansas during the war. Frank's younger brother Jesse joined them and became a cold-eyed killer within a short time. Quantrill's group is responsible for gunning down 200 men and boys during the raid on Lawrence, Kansas. Bloody Bill Anderson also had a group of raiders, but neither he nor Quantrill's group were ever recognized by the Confederacy as authorized troops. That means they always were outlaws, bushwhackers, though considered heroes by Missourians, many of whom were their extended kin. After the war, they were quite used to gunning men down in cold blood and taking what they wanted and simply continued to do so.

Other outlaws fed from the East, drawn West for one reason or another. Sometimes it was the freedom from the constraints of the eastern cities. Both Billy the Kid and the Sundance Kid hailed from the East.

Who might these outlaws be (other than anyone you invent, that is)? Well, beyond the already mentioned Billy the Kid, we have the Clantons who shot it out with the Earps and Doc Holiday in Tombstone in 1881. Besides Jesse and Frank James and their cousin Cole Younger and his kin, there's Black Bart in Northern California. Curly Bill Brocus, The Sundance Kid, Butch Cassidy, John Wesley Hardin, Tom Horn (who was once a Pinkerton operative) and a host of others. Sometimes a few of these were outlaws, sometimes they were lawmen, but often, they were all gamblers.

Don't discount the con artists as possible characters or character models. Jefferson "Soapy" Smith is the "greatest" of these, making himself king of crime and vice in Denver, then Creede, Colorado, before moving on to Skagway, Alaskan Territory when the Klondike/Yukon gold strikes were the latest get-rich-quick location in 1898.

Same goes for gamblers. The professional ones weren't likely to be involved holding up stages, but certainly in cleaning the pockets of those who sat down opposite them for a hand of cards or roll of the dice. There were lawmen who made a side living, if not a career, at the tables. Wyatt Earp was partial owner in a couple saloons. Doc Holiday, a consumptive dentist from back East, made his living at the tables. Wild Bill Hickok not only played regularly, but he was also killed at a poker table the day that gambling fever overcame his personal safety rule to keep his back to a wall. Poker Alice was the most famous of the lady gamblers.

The old west could be an equalizer for there were female outlaws as well. Frequently they were cattle rustlers (Cattle Kate, for one) or girlfriends or wives or pseudo-wives of male outlaws, like Etta Place who was the Sundance Kid's main squeeze. Some of these ladies were captured, jailed and a few hanged from the nearest sturdy tree branch by riled up citizens.

Oddly enough, although American outlaws apparently had a trail to escape authorities that lead from Canada to Mexico, no names surfaced in a search for 19th century outlaws, bank robbers, or train hold ups in Canada. Apparently, those Mounties kept things under their hats when they went after culprits. There is a book, *Outlaws and Lawmen of Western Canada* by Heritage House, that should supply some details should you be steaming through British Columbia.

The same problem did not occur when it comes to our Down Under locations.

In Australia they called outlaws "bushrangers." The heyday for these fellows was 1850 through the 1860s when the gold rush was on. Easy pickings as transportation was by hoof, wagon, and foot, the constabulary was shorthanded because so many men had debunked to the gold fields, and the things stolen were easy to unload.

There had been bushrangers earlier than this, of course, and there were some in the later decades as well. Earlier they'd been convicts who slipped the leash and had the survival know-how to live in the bush. By the 1860s and 1870s, the background of the bushrangers had changed. They were now the sons of ex-convicts looking for adventure, danger and a profitable good time. Their stomping grounds tended to be in New South Wales around the Lachlan Valley, Forbes, Yass and Cowra.

Some of the bushrangers who made a name for themselves and got in the history books are: Frank Gardiner, John Gilbert, Ben Hall, and Mad Dog Dan Morgan (aka John Fuller). Ned Kelly had a gang that included his brother, and in 1906 had his story flickering on Australian movie screens. Jack Donahue had the sort of reputation that led someone to write a ballad about him. Michael Howe was a bushranger in Tasmania. Captain Thunderbolt holds the longevity record, being a pain in law enforcement's neck for six and a half years before he was shot in 1870. Captain Starlight used the name Frank Pearson when in New South Wales and Harry Redford when he was in Queensland. He was arrested but not convicted at his trial. He died either in 1899 or 1901 – it depends on what name you find him listed under.

Business began to be bad for bushrangers in the later 1870s and onwards because there were far more people settling in their old stomping grounds, much better transportation, and improved police forces.

New Zealand appears to have been quite peaceful – where outlaws are concerned. At least for the period leading into and out of the 1870s and 1880s.

Let's head back to the States and look in on two places that qualify as urban settings though they are most definitely within the Weird West.

Weird Urban West
The Gilded Age

There really isn't an official Steampunk term for stories that take place in the urban settings of the Weird West countries, but they shouldn't be called Victorian per se. Even Gilded Age doesn't entirely suit them for places like San Francisco were boom cities in earlier decades. Thus, this section is termed Weird Urban West. While we'll concentrate on the Gilded Age, these cities West of the Mississippi River are places where Steampunk opportunities abound for us!

San Francisco

The City by the Bay, San Francisco is the town to benefit most — and first — in a big way from a mining strike. It takes no time at all to be the first and *only* place large enough to merit the term "city" west of the Mississippi. Not that any of the gold was *in* Frisco (as it was called fondly by residents and visitors alike originally). No, what Frisco had was the sweetest little harbor possible for ocean arrival of both supplies and folks. But its birth is back in that earliest of western mining strikes in 1848. By the Gilded Age, San Francisco had everything — including attitude — many an Eastern city might envy.

So much money had poured into the city through mining, railroads, and merchandise that the lifestyle improved by leaps and bounds. Bachelors as well as visitors took up residence in hotels. The Palace was a great place to stay by the 1870s, if you could afford it. The mansions had begun to fill the sides of Nob Hill, despite the climb (oh, but what a view!). The harbor packed with stranded ships of 1850 had cleared out — or been cleared out — and transportation in and out of the city was moving along nicely. The railroad barons had ensured train travel was possible from San Francisco clear across the Nation.

In 1854 San Franciscans had been worked up over the arrival of 780 Chinese (200 of them female) aboard the *Lord Warriston*, but there was an established Chinatown at the foot of Nob Hill by the Gilded Age.

Because the town had been so flammable in the earlier decades, fire-proof buildings were plentiful. Nob Hill was crowded with mansions despite the fact that the notorious Barbary Coast vice district lay at its foot. The "Frisco" of the early years was moving ever closer to insisting it was "San Francisco", no pet names need apply for the Paris of the Pacific Coast.

Horse-drawn cars (from 1860) and cable cars (from 1873) made it possible to get up and down the many hills. The Market Street Railway began as a horse car line, opening on July 4, 1860. Within a few years the horses were replaced by steam and the mass-transit system consisted of an engine that was a hybrid of locomotive and passenger car that had enough power to pull another car behind it. The steep slope of those hills had to be murder on animal and steam engine alike though and in 1873 the first cable drawn car went into service as the Clay Street Hill Railroad, but replacing all the horse-drawn lines took some time — and ready cash. Soon there were five cable lines hauling folks and goods with a cable car leaving the Ferry Building every 15 seconds during rush hour traffic!

Progress rushes on and in 1895 the Southern Pacific Railroad was converting everything to electric streetcars and selling off the cable cars. If you want to rush progress and get vehicles running on gasoline engines tooling around the streets earlier than the turn of the century, be aware that Fireman's Fund might be talked into selling automobile insurance prior to when they did historically. One of their salesmen was given the first company car in 1902, a Stevens Duryea, Stanhope model, that had a crank and engine under the front seat and was steered not with a driver's wheel but with a lever. What is Steampunk worthy here is that the car he was driving had been advertised as being "built like a watch." It had two "speeds" — basically moving or at a full stop. It went forward and in reverse and shifting into any gear required depended on a cam, but when the cam nuts loosened it was to a blacksmith the Stanhope went. There weren't any auto repair garages yet and gasoline was purchased at a drug store, where it ran 60 cents a gallon (the equivalent of $15.62 a gallon in 2014). Hardware and paint stores could usually supply gasoline, too, though you had to carry two five-gallon cans to put the gasoline in plus a third gallon can to carry a reserve of oil. Surely a Steampunk mechanic can come up with something a bit jiffier...or something like the Duryea Stanhope earlier.

When it comes to underground systems, San Francisco didn't begin considering one until 1918, but that doesn't mean you can't have one in Steampunk San Francisco far earlier.

If we use the Victorian urban Steampunk stories as a model, one of the places frequently visited by one or more characters is the red-light district. In San Francisco, probably the most famous of these is the Barbary Coast. Its roots are firmly sunk in that notoriously deep mud of the earliest years of the city. It was really a very compact area, a mere nine blocks. The area was bounded by Montgomery, Washington and Stockton streets and Broadway. Pacific Avenue was particularly well known and an easy road to travel as it led from the wharfs. This was where a man with money in his pocket wanted to be if his interest was in gambling (which was illegal except in private clubs by the 1870s), in sharing it with a lovely more than willing to bounce the mattress with him, and if he had anything left at the close of the evening, to take the risk of being robbed of as crime was rampant in the area. In earlier years the Coast had its share of opium dens but as Chinatown grew these had probably changed their addresses to Dupont Street (which was changed to Grant Street after the 1906 Earthquake required rebuilding of the area). The Barbary Coast doesn't suffer for clients until it burns to the ground in the wake of the 1906 fires, and even then, it bounces back for a few years. But they aren't our target years, so let's move on.

San Francisco was the first city to have a telephone directory. Oh, sure, New Haven, Connecticut had one a few months before (February 1878 to be exact) the San Francisco one was printed (June 1, 1878), but New Haven's was small, a mere two sheets of paper. There were 173 listings for businesses in San Francisco's first phone directory. It doesn't give phone numbers – they weren't being used yet since you rang the operator and told them who you wanted to talk to in these extremely early years of telephone service – but it does have names and addresses and the type of business. One of those businesses on the telephone exchange was The California

Electric Company, though it wasn't until 1888 that an electric street light is installed in front of City Hall and demands for electricity in businesses and homes are on the rise.

San Francisco has something in common with London as a setting. It has fog for atmosphere. But because its history begins and grows quickly thanks to Industrial Revolution creations and the greed of men newly rich to work with, San Francisco is perfect Weird Urban West territory.

Denver

Denver, Queen of the West, like so many of the mining era cities, owes its beginnings to gold. It was founded in 1858 nearly in sync with the ore finds on nearby Pike's Peak. The 1860s weren't a kind time for little Denver City. Not only did the U.S. government sorta forget they existed because the focus back east was on beating the South into submission, but the city endured fire, flood and transportation difficulties. But Denver City became the territorial capital in 1865 and decided that the best way to get famous was to drop its last name. Colorado won statehood in 1876 with Denver as the temporary state capital until getting the job full time in 1881.

Located as it was where Cherry Creek meets the South Platte River, flooding was an occasional problem in 1875 and 1878 in Denver. Fires in the early decades had led to more and more brick and "fire-proof" structures being built, though that didn't stop the city from being visited by fire. On its own, Denver had grown but to continue progressing it had reached the point where it needed one last thing to truly merit "city" status: a railroad.

Building one or being involved in the details revolving around the laying of the rails sounds like an excellent employment opportunity for Steampunk characters or minions from their workshops, or a challenge for a forward-thinking Steampunk engineer.

Denver's citizens had been crushed when the Union Pacific bypassed them, choosing to lay rails toward Cheyenne, 100 miles to the north, in the late 1860s. So, they decided to build their own railroad. Fund raising began in earnest and $300,000 was collected. It took more than that to get progress bound their way so in January 1868 voters approved a $500,000 bond. Men reported for work to begin laying rail in May. But first, you'll not be surprised to learn, everyone celebrated the groundbreaking with speeches, songs and kegs of beer. The Denver Pacific would do them proud. On June 24, 1870 there was cause for another celebration as the final spike was behind them.

The Denver Pacific did exactly what everyone wanted it to do. New residents arrived, tourists arrived, supplies arrived. Throughout the 1870s an average of 100 newcomers arrived to settle in Denver every day – say, 3,000 a month. Only 4,759 citizens had called Denver home in 1870 but by 1880 there were more than 35,000. By 1890 there were over 100,000. When Oscar Wilde visited in the 1880s, he said Denver was "one of the few cities in the world where practically none of the adult residents were native-born."

Foreign arrivals were overwhelmingly German, and they tended to do very well in Denver. Approximately 16 of the 48 saloons were owned by natives of Germany or Austria in 1880. These premises offered selections from sauerkraut, strudel and beer to other elements of German culture, including newspapers in German. In 1873 a $1,000 orchestrion was installed in the Orchestrion Hall. What is an "orchestrion"? It's an 11-foot tall machine that incorporates horns, reeds, xylophone and drums. It took a week to put together. There were numerous breweries and bottlers supplying 410 saloons (offering nickel beer and free lunches) in Denver when the new century was in full swing – all going out of business the day prohibition started in 1920.

There were also Irish (3% of the population and the most prolific word is) who benefited by going west to Denver since there were no "No Irish Need Apply" signs in the city like there were all along the Eastern seaboard. But then there were plenty of other people to be discriminated against and distrusted on the streets of Denver. They were easy to spot for they had red, brown, yellow or black skin. The 19th century's Nativist mindset was very prejudicial.

The English made up the 3rd largest group of foreigners. Railroads, like the Denver & Rio Grande, were financed by British concerns. British mining firms – 25 of them – were in place by 1890. The British also took to ranching since they were a nation that enjoyed beef. For our Steampunk purposes the British work well since they arrived from the birthplace of the Industrial Revolution, but also because they were instrumental in planning and financing the High Line Canal. This rerouted the South Platte's water, taking it on an 88-mile long run though the agricultural land south and east of Denver. In fact, the High Line was also known in town as the "English Ditch." $550,000 later it was up and running in 1882 and did exactly what it was supposed to do – increased the size of Denver and Aurora, the suburb to the south.

Should the Denver area interest you as a setting for your Steampunk tale, peopling it with characters of German, Irish, and English descent as well as Americans from the East will represent historic Denver nicely.

It wasn't merely the railroad and the scenery that brought newcomers to Denver, though. It was silver. The gold fields were part of history in the 1880s when silver began a new rush. There had always been silver in the hills, but the low price of silver ore discouraged miners from pursuing it. That changed with the passing of the Bland-Allison Act in 1878 which authorized the free coinage of silver. Leadville boomed into a city of 40,000 by 1880, but it was to Denver that the riches flowed. To Denver that the newly rich moved. Among them was Horace Tabor, whose richly appointed opera house reveled in the opulence of the Gilded Age. In 1893 the ten storied Brown Palace Hotel opened. Tabor's Grand, at 16th and Curtis streets, flabbergasted Denverites with its eclectic and extravagant style. The Tabor Grand Saloon was considered the finest bar in town. It also had the drawing card of possessing an all ladies orchestra.

1893 spelled financial panic, not just in Denver but across the nation as the silver boom lost its hustle thanks to the passage of the Sherman Act which put the U.S. back on the gold standard. With the loss of silver wealth eighteen banks closed in July 1893 in Denver, though others, like the Colorado National Bank, survived because they hadn't put their entire focus on the mining industry. The price of silver dropped from $1 an ounce to around 50 cents an ounce and silver mining, Colorado's premier industry, tumbled. More money had been sunk in mines than was ever pried from the rock.

Of Steampunk note, there was a strange machine found among the confiscated property. Created by the Chlorination and Cyanide

Supply Company was a metal tube-like machine built for "extracting gold, silver, copper and platinum from their respective or mixed ores.'" Or so the label claimed. Sounds like a creation from a Steampunk machine shop, doesn't it? Well, with a few tweaks to make even better, perhaps.

Fortunately, Denver hadn't been built on the fortunes in the mines after those early days. The railroad, agricultural, manufacturing and even food processing were its lodestones now. It was the 26th largest city in the U.S., with nearly all the cities above it being east of the Mississippi. In 1890 it ranked 3rd, just behind San Francisco and Omaha, on the list for west of the Mississippi. It had beaten out Omaha in population figures by 1900, and the population then doubled from 1900 to 1920.

With prosperity comes corruption though and the 1880s and 1890s featured underworld bosses, the most famous probably being Soapy Smith, mentioned back in the *Outlaw* section. Gambling and other vices and criminal activities were rampant with city officials and the police taking handouts to look the other way. Bordellos for the wealthy and for the poor, but equally hungry for vice, could be found. The best places were run by Mattie Silks and Jenny Rogers but a stumble along Market Street not far from them were the cribs of the lowest rung prostitutes. Edward Chase had several gambling establishments and in 1880, if a ranking had been issued, Denver's vice district would have fallen in third place, just below San Francisco's Barbary Coast and New Orleans' Storyville. If you were new in town and looking for a bit of naughty fun, many of the vice dens were only a few steps away and if they didn't suit you there were guidebooks sold at newsstands where other addresses for similar delights could be found.

How fast can you say dystopian situation? The vice lords would certainly keep their employees under such a stern thumb, wouldn't they?

Not all entertainment was of the sordid or vice laden type though. There was opera and stages that catered to the famous traveling players and singers of the day. For the not as well-known there was a variety of other theatres most of which didn't stay in business long. And if the audience that visited these latter venues was not to your liking, Denver churches frequently had musical evenings anyone could enjoy in the later part of the century.

The first hotel that caters to those who like the best was the Windsor, a British backed concern, as was the Oxford. There were cricket matches at the Albion Club to entertain (and confuse those whose backgrounds were cricket-less) in the 1880s. And for Gilded Age homes there are Queen Anne and English Revival styled mansions in the districts like Capitol Hill.

However, the Bottoms, down near the South Platte River, was an area unfit for either proper Englishman or Denverite. It was on a flood plain and the railroad ran through it. It was considered a slum area, but incoming Italian peasant farmers found the place had good soil for farming as well as the convenience of nearby water and settled in.

Denver residents were able to hop on horse-drawn streetcar lines in the 1870s but in 1886 the Denver Tramway Company secured exclusive right to build electric streetcar lines. By 1900 the D.T.C. had a monopoly, having driven the competition out of business. They now offered city-wide lines of trolleys running on networks of overhead electric lines. They became one of Denver's largest employers as the majority of residents hopped on a streetcar when headed to work, out for shopping or for whatever entertainment beckoned. There were even special cars available for hire for weddings and funerals.

It was the religious communities of Denver that coordinated their charities to best help the city's poor in 1887 and inadvertently founded what would later become the United Way.

In 1893 Colorado took a leap that the nation itself wouldn't make for another 27 years – it granted the vote to women in the state. This might be important to your Steampunk heroine even if she can't vote in national elections, she can belly up to the ballot box for local and state ones. Feel all empowered and modern.

Denver and San Francisco are the most logical urban centers for Weird Urban West storylines simply because they have much in common with the smaller communities west of the Mississippi. They grew quickly and had their share of mining and railroad related growth spurts as well as crime and natural disasters to create dystopian settings. If there is going to be a wealthy mastermind looking to take over a profitable proportion of the West, chances are they'd call one of these two cities home.

But not all urban Steampunk settings are tied to what was happening beyond the Mississippi. A good number of opportunities await us East of the Big Muddy.

Weird East
Gilded Age

There isn't a category termed Weird East...yet...in the Steampunk world, but there really should be. *This* is where the Gilded Age really reigns, particularly in the large and industrial cities, the transportation hubs. So, we're going to take a stroll through four of the best bets for a Steampunk story setting. And we'll begin with the most western of these . . .

Chicago
Oddly enough, in the early 1900s Chicago was considered a western city. Strange considering it is now considered a Midwestern city, but then even Cincinnati was a "western city" at the turn of the century. Well, it was west of the Alleghenies.

While not as old as those eastern seaboard places, Chicago is old by most Midwestern standards. As a city it crawled from beneath ye olde cabbage leaf (that is how cities are born, right?) in 1832. Sure there had been folks visiting and living on the spot prior to that but we're concerned with Chicago itself, not the locale.

A lot of roads lead to Chicago, a lot of ships arrived in Chicago via the Great Lakes and barges via the Illinois and Michigan Canal, and it became a railroad hub. Livestock from hogs to cattle arrived in Chicago for slaughter and salting before pushing off along the rails and in the ships bound for points East. This market got even bigger in 1870 when refrigerated train cars could ship fresh rather than preserved meat East.

R.W. Sears started his retail catalog in 1888 in Wisconsin, but he moved to Chicago in 1889 and in 1893 partnered up with Mr. Roebuck. It was even possible to purchase automobiles made in Chicago through the catalog from 1905 to 1915. He hadn't originated the idea of shopping from home because Aaron Montgomery Ward, a traveling salesman (or drummer, as they were known back when, considering they were "drumming" up business for the firm they represented), went to press with his first catalog in 1872 – it was one page long and offered 162 items and included ordering instructions. By 1883 people were calling Montgomery Ward's the "Wish Book" and perusing a 240-page catalog of 10,000 items. Don't you wonder what your Steampunk characters could get via these catalogues to put together their mechanical minions or some other handy device?

Travelers arriving in town weren't very kind though – they called Chicago "the filthiest city in America". Well, there was this prairie bog area that insects liked to visit, and disease and mud were par for the course. In the early years horses got stuck in the mud in the spring but a few folks had enough of a sense of humor to post signs that said "'Fastest route to China'" and "'No Bottom Here'" in dangerous areas. The city fathers decided something needed to be done and high on their list was sewage pipes. Steampunk engineers can supply their own plans for reworking these systems, of course.

Another event just crying for Steampunk engineering will take us out of the Gilded Age but it's great backstory. That is the decision in 1856 to elevate the entire city by four to five feet. The plan was to use a new process of jacking buildings up. In the case of the Brigg's Hotel, which weighed 22,000 tons and was five stories tall, the proprietors didn't bother to close their doors while the building was lifted but stayed open for business. They might as well have used magic to accomplish the feat, it was that astonishing!

Chicago holds the record for growth, moving from the few hundred souls that put down roots there in 1832 to being the second most populated city (299,000 people) in the United States in 1870 (New York City was #1). By 1900 there were 1.7 million people living in Chicago, making it the fastest growing city of all time.

In 1856 a Scots emigrant, a former cooper who ended up working for the police, decided to go it on his own and opened the Pinkerton Detective Agency in Chicago. By the Gilded Age they were the private security firm big business turned to. Their business and operatives (Allan didn't like the term "detective") work well for Steampunk because...

- they were very successful in what they did

- they were at the forefront in covert operations with the successful infiltration of the coal miners' union, and the unsuccessful (and fatal for several operatives) attempts to infiltrate the James Gang

- their work with and for the railroads as express guards and strike breakers

- and their use of female operatives

All excellent Steampunk scenarios or jobs for your characters.

There was this little problem of a fire in 1871, of course. The part about Mrs. O'Leary's cow – well, sorry, it's fictional, but the O'Leary barn was the first treat tasted by the fire of October 8 through October 10 (Sunday evening 9 p.m. into Tuesday before it was out). The tally in loses were 300 dead, 18,000 buildings destroyed and 3.3 miles of the city ready for major renewal projects. The problem had been that common to the western towns that were visited frequently by fire – so many things were constructed of wood: buildings, sidewalks and even streets paved with planks. They all tended to catch fire and pass it along to the next block down. The new city was built under new and far more detailed fire-safety codes, one of which emphasized constructions of masonry rather than of wood. Different materials for pavements were also in order.

Because the cause of the fire was never determined, this is definitely Steampunk possibility territory – either in how it was started (or why depending on a villain's goals), but also for a heroic effort in Steampunk technology in putting out the fire...or clearing the rubble...or building the new structures. And they weren't quite "skyscrapers" yet historically, but that doesn't stop us from building things taller than they were. It's all in the tools and materials, isn't it? And Chicago is the home of the first official "skyscraper", the Home Insurance Building, which opened for business with ten stories in 1885.

From disaster we move on to a celebration of wonders – The World's Columbian Exposition of 1893. Little Egypt did her dance there and shocked many. All the buildings were white, which resulted in the area being called The White City. It featured the first Ferris wheel and had the first midway at an exposition. There was also a serial killer at large: H.H. Holmes.

Looking for someone more fiendish than a serial killer? Well, to modern eyes, perhaps. How about the "father of modern advertising", Albert Lasker, who made Chicago his home from 1898 to 1942, so he's over into the Progressive Era rather than the Gilded Age, but we'll make an exception because he could be a model for a Steampunk Gilded Age character. The ads Lasker wrote were manipulative for he saw the modern woman as an untapped market for selling cigarettes and told them that smoking Lucky Strikes was an excellent way to keep weight off. If he could put that kind of spin on things, just think what he could sell folks on for his Steampunk client, be they good or bad.

Prior to the fire of 1871 the neighborhoods where characters should head to indulge in a bit of vice are along Clark Street, one of those most disreputable being the Little Cheyenne area between Van Buren and Congress. (In retaliation, in Cheyenne there was a similar district known as Little Chicago.) Other sections were known as Hell's Half Acre, Coop's Holler, Satan's Mile, the Bad Lands, Dead Man's Alley, and Noah's Ark, which was owned by a city alderman. The red-light district was located directly in the 1871 fire's path, but the bordellos and gambling halls were back in business soon after the embers cooled.

When the Columbian Exposition came to town in 1893, a new world of vice was already established to welcome visitors and stayed open into the new century. The South Side "Levee" District fell within the borders of 18th and 22nd Streets between State and Armour. Within these blocks could be found nearly 40 brothels, an equal number of saloons, gambling halls and an opium den.

Prior to the 1871 Fire, the city's wealthy built mansions along Michigan Avenue, but the fire decimated the area. Wreckage from the area was used to fill in the shoreline so that in the 20th century nearly a quarter mile had been gained. Since rebuilding appeared to be out of the question for some, those with money turned to Prairie Avenue where a number of mansions were built from the 1870s into the 1890s, and The Gold Coast, both historic districts today.

Successful Steampunk characters can reside in these neighborhoods and still be nefarious types if you choose.

In 1877 a 10% wage cut for railroad men lead to a nationwide strike as numerous other workers sided with the strikers, particularly after labor union agitators and socialist sympathizers began working up the crowds of men. This was the first major strike in the United States. It worked its way from the East coast to the shores of Lake Michigan. When the mob of railroad, meatpacking and lumber men faced off with security forces that included six companies of soldiers from the U.S. Army, 18 men died in the scuffle. There is probably a profit to be made by a Steampunk villain from this event – or by a writer putting a Steampunk spin on it.

One of the things that Chicago is known for is the stockyards. It was where Texas beef on the hoof was shipped when the cattle driven to the railheads stepped aboard a train. The Chicago Union Stock Yards and Armor Packing facilities could serve as settings or models should you wish to mix a bit of Weird rural West with Weird urban eastern Steampunk

And how did the city come by its moniker of the Windy City? Oddly enough it wasn't because the wind blew down through the concrete and brick canyons of the streets. It was what the New York newspapers called the city based on the boastfulness of the politicians and lobbyists from Chicago during the Gilded Age.

Pittsburg

Pittsburg? Not exactly one of the cities you thought we'd visit with Steampunk in mind? Well, it's not only an old town, it's an industrial town – *the* Industrial Town.

The natural resources in the area lend themselves to industry for Pittsburg is at the center of one of the busiest coalfields in the U.S. There is also oil, natural gas, lumber, and the combined waterpower of the Monongahela and the Allegheny rivers joining to create the wide expanse of the Ohio River at Pittsburg.

While it dates back to the French and Indian war when there was a fort built at the junction of the rivers, by 1857 there were ten thousand workers employed by over nine hundred factories, and they were turning out nearly $12 million in goods with the help of four hundred steam engines. Those engines burned twenty-two million bushels of coal to melt a hundred and twenty-seven thousand tons of iron. Although it was an inland city using rivers, rails and roads to ship products, it was the third busiest port in the nation. New York was #1 and New Orleans #2, and both are located on ocean shores. All of this supplies us with opportunities for our Steampunk characters in Pittsburg.

Around 1859 the Iron City morphed into the Steel City and dominated industry in pre-Civil War America. This was the year that coke-fire smelting iron furnaces were introduced by the Clinton and Soho factory. When the war arrived, armaments contracts flew into the Allegheny Arsenal and the Fort Pitt Foundry. Iron-clad warships and the first 21" long gun shipped from Pittsburg. By 1865 half of the steel and a third of the glass produced in the U.S. was created in Pittsburg furnaces. And all of this is *before* our Gilded Age era!

The 1870s give Pittsburg even more to crow about. Names still recognized today made fortunes in the industries of Pittsburgh: Carnegie, Frick, Mellon, Schwab, and Westinghouse. In the 1870s the factories of Pittsburg were no longer small, they were giant conglomerations for mass production using "modern management organization"...well, modern for the time, though this is where the seeds of current business organization sprang to life. In 1875 the Edgar Thomson Works was making steel rail for the railroads using the Bessemer process.

We talked about immigrants elsewhere. Well, it should be no surprise that, like the other communities we've visited, the folks who crossed the "pond" to settle in Pittsburg were largely from Germany and Ireland (many Scots-Irish). One of those German immigrants' sons started his own company in 1872 – the H. J. Heinz Company, where they were soon offering fifty-seven varieties of tinned goods. Heinz was involved in reform to improve food purity, and though he was adamantly against labor unions, he was involved in improving workers' wages, hours, and the conditions in which they worked.

Remember how in 1877 railroad workers across the eastern half of the country (from Chicago back to the Atlantic cities) went on strike due to wage cuts? Pittsburgh, being a transportation hub, had its share of rioting during the time, the result of which was the burning of Pennsylvania Railroad's Union Station. Another forty some buildings were also set afire and dozens of people died. In 1892 the Homestead Strike had a smaller number of casualties: three Pinkerton detectives sent in to break up the strike and seven striking workers.

Things, as always, returned to normal and in 1890 Gilded Age steel magnate Andrew Carnegie began his philanthropic work by building libraries in small towns around the nation. It was the same year that trolleys appeared on the streets in Pittsburgh.

Pittsburgh supplies everything the mad Steampunk inventor (and the not so mad one) requires to build fantastic machines. The only transportation type that appears to be missing in this hub city is that by air…well, at least in the 19th century. You can always fix that in your version of Steampunk Pittsburgh though. There are foundries galore and money seems to pour into the coffers. All those Gilded Era millionaires loading up their bank accounts via Pittsburgh industry seem to prove that. Innovation was alive and well – Heinz is an excellent example of this – so as an urban environment to found your Steampunk empire, the city on the banks of three rivers, a canal, a turnpike, and numerous railway lines sounds like location, location, location!

Boston

Boston is a Goldilocks town because it wasn't the first pick of the Puritan colonists arriving in 1630. They tried two other locations before finding a spot to unpack their luggage. This area featured three hills, so they named the town Trimountaine. Really deep thinkers, these Puritans. Later it was renamed Boston.

And those three hills? There is only one left – Beacon Hill. The other two were "dismantled" to use as fill to make more viable building areas over the years.

By the 1870s Boston might be strait-laced compared to some cities but it has numerous theatres and other entertainments. The Cyclorama Building goes up in 1884. Cycloramas are extremely popular until the first "moving" pictures push them aside. The Boston Pops Orchestra is established in 1885, and the Boston Marathon is first run on April 19, 1897. The Boston Red Sox team isn't founded until 1901 though.

GEARED UP WRITING STEAMPUNK

In June of 1872 the World's Peace Jubilee and International Musical Festival was hosted in Boston. In 1880, you can attend the Globe Theatre, the Boston Theatre, the Park Theatre, the Boylston Museum (where they feature "The Great Dime Show") or the Boston Museum. Hint, the "museums" were theatres, too. In September of 1882 it is possible to see "real genuine western Indians" from six different tribes at the Indian Village set up across from the Boston and Portsmouth Depot. As an added feature, "The Trapper's Daughter" was performed. Melodrama at its best, no doubt. The first vaudeville theatre opened in 1883. Head to the Notman Photography Studio to have your picture taken, it's located on Boylston Street near the Public Garden in 1884. And at Young's Hotel, Mr. Charles Hill sat down to eat a dinner of crow to honor a bet on the Presidential election. His candidate had lost. Yes, that's a strange thing to add in here, but it seems like a great opening for a Steampunk story, placing Mr. Hill in a position where he might want to have a spot of revenge in mind and cause the Cleveland administration some headaches. Since Cleveland was the 22nd President for 1885 to 1889 and the 24th President from 1893 to 1897, the choice of when to enact that revenge is up to the perpetrator.

The Great Boston Fire of 1872 on the evening of November 9 results in the loss of 776 buildings and 30 people. There is a Thanksgiving Day fire in 1889 which kills two firemen. For those engaged in adding crime to their Steampunk mix, it might help to know that part of the problem with this particular fire was that buildings were over insured, and arson was frequent.

At mid-century the police department was reorganized using the template perfected by Scotland Yard. For a few decades the men on the force used the telegraph to communicate between an area station and the central office but replaced the tapped-out messages in 1878 with telephones, using them on a trial basis at first. The telephone, of course, was invented in Boston, with the first phone call made between Alexander Graham Bell and his friend Thomas Watson occurring in 1876.

The first steam fireboat in Boston went into service in 1873 as did a "self-propelled steam engine towing hose reel". Electric firehouse gongs were up and ringing in 1882. The first electric streetlamps are installed at Scolly Square in 1882 as well, but the last of the gas lamps won't disappear until 1914. The first subway opened in 1897: The Tremont Street Subway.

Boston's traditional upper class, particularly during the Gilded Age, were termed the Boston Brahmins. If they didn't live on Beacon Hill, they lived in Cambridge to be near Harvard.

Your heroine might find a place to stay at the YWCA soon after 1867, the year it was incorporated. Harvard, of course, has been around forever, well, since 1636, but in the mid-19th century the curriculum was *really* old hat there. Mentioned before but worth a second touting is The Massachusetts Institute of Technology (M.I.T.), founded in 1861. It didn't exactly open for students until after the Civil War...so many of the boys being off to war and all. The emphasis was on engineering, chemistry, and other sciences rather than the classics. Obvious place for Steampunk characters to attend school, isn't it? And among the male students at the new college was a woman: Ellen Swallow Richards.

By the Gilded Age immigrants have streamed into Boston. Oddly enough, the city attracts many Chinese as well as Irish, with representatives of other European nations setting up their own neighborhoods as well. And among the Irish immigrants were men who, if they were fortunate enough to join the wealthy middle class, tended to bankroll the Fenians back in Ireland and London in their terrorist activities. Now *that* is a cross over between Weird East and Victorian Steampunk worlds!

New York

If you thought that New York City was the #1 city in the world, think again. Throughout the 19th century the largest city in the world was...(BUZZZZ)...London. Yep, London...in England.

But we're dealing with the U.S. right now and the undisputed champ here was (at least from 1835 on) New York City.

While they started working on it in 1853, Central Park (59th to 110th streets between 5th and 8th avenues) wasn't completed until 1873 as the city stretched further north. Frederick Law Olmstead and Calvert Vaux's "Greensward Plan" is a Steampunk opportunity for an ongoing event that could be turned to your own purposes. What they used to create the place can be built upon, enlarged, made awesomely fantastic. Remember, in any Steampunk book, the "world" your characters inhabit is just as important as any nefarious device built by someone attempting to take over the world...or merely New York City, as the case may be. Central Steampunk Park is where characters can stroll, enjoy various entertainments, or arrange to meet contacts.

In building the real park the crews used gunpowder, more than had been used at the Battle of Gettysburg, to clear the area. It was a project that called for a huge number of laborers with shovels, and Olmstead and Vaux brought in the latest in steam-powered equipment plus wheeled tree moving machines custom designed for the job. Absolutely perfect for tweaking those steam-powered machines. This may be right up your character's alley. Once all the dirt had been moved around and the forest tamed, grass was planted. It was kept trimmed by a flock of sheep from the 1860s into the Depression of the 1930s when city officials feared they'd be nabbed by the destitute for meals. This means you could have sheep trimming the greenery during the Steampunk Gilded Age, or you could replace them with your own mechanical nibblers.

To many there appeared to be only two classes of people in New York during the Gilded Age: the rich and the poor. If your characters are fortunate enough to be among the wealthy or have a reason for visiting them in their homes, they could be headed for a townhouse or a mansion. The mansions, of course, are located on Park Avenue and Fifth Avenue. Most of them are gone today, replaced by skyscrapers, but once the area was graced by the Vanderbilts, Astors, Schawbs, the Bradley Martins, and the Carnegies. The Brokaw mansion appeared to be a misplaced castle, the steps to the front door looking more like they should be crossing a moat than be part of an inner-city property. In a bow to what a Steampunk heroine could concoct for her wardrobe, Alva Vanderbilt threw a masquerade where she came as "Electric Light", her white satin gown trimmed with diamonds and wired with batteries so that she could light it up.

There were far more in the "poor" category than the "rich" one, naturally. By the 1850s one-fourth of New York City was Irish. Ergo, you'd be sadly lacking to leave the sons of Erin out of a Steampunk tale. They ran most of the gangs in the city – Five Points area ring any bells? How about the Dead Rabbits, the name of one of the gangs...actually, the most infamous and possibly longest thriving one.

Some of the gangs specialized in river piracy, others in picking pockets, and still others in anything that would pay. The earliest gangs were in existence in the early 1800s, but which gang was top of the pack changed over time. The Boodle Gang was formed in the 1850s and was still active in the 1890s. The Dead Rabbits were involved in a riot in 1857 and though made up mostly of those of Irish descent, by the early 20th century had incorporated incoming Italians, who went on to form the early Mafia groups of the Roaring Twenties. The Tenth Avenue Gang was notorious for pulling off the first train robbery in Manhattan on the Hudson Line in 1868. The Tub of Blood Bunch operated on the waterfront into the 1880s. There were non-Irish gangs, too, though ethnicity still was a main feature for the Yiddish Black Hand, which was active until around 1913, and the Four Brothers Tongs, Hip Sing Association and the On Leong Tong. The Yiddish Black Hand gang had a rate sheet. Arranging a fatal shooting ran $500; a non-fatal shooting was $100; poisoning a team of horses $50; poisoning one horse $35; and stealing a horse and rig ran $25.

The Five Points area in New York City was already a slum in the 1820s, but it was also a business area with gambling dens, brothels and frequent muggings. Charles Dickens visited the Five Points neighborhood while on a speaking tour in 1842 and was appalled at the squalor of the area. Decades later, that hadn't changed.

The Five Points area was the equal of the East End slums of London though it appears to have held the record for the number of murders committed, held it for 70 years. It was also an area where cholera was a frequent visitor that then spread out into the surrounding area to creep through the city. This is another dystopian element that could be used for a Steampunk tale set in 19th century New York City.

Five Points isn't the only "downside" in the city though. The Tenderloin was vice and entertainment central from around 1876 into the early 20th century – 23rd Street to 42nd Street from Fifth Avenue to Seventh Avenue, then expanding up toward 62nd and over to Eighth Avenue. Think Garment District, Theatre District, and thereabouts on a modern map. The Tenderloin hosted "the largest number of nightclubs, saloons, bordellos, gambling casinos, [and] dance halls" leading reformers to term the area Satan's Circus. A gent looking for an eyeful could catch a performance of the can-can at the Haymarket on Sixth Avenue below 30th Street, or view "sex exhibitions...in the balconies"...or engage in "discreet sex" with one of the house prostitutes in a curtained-off gallery. Shocking! And typically, dark side Victorian.

The railroad changed some things when the Hudson River Railroad came to town. In 1851 it was possible to travel by rail all the way to Albany from the end of the line at 60th Street along 11th Avenue. Industry followed with tanneries now dumping vats in the river and shipping products out along the line. The docks also offered jobs to the newly arrived immigrants. After the Civil War the population boomed, more tenements went up, immigration reached new highs and the area became more one of poverty. Hell's Kitchen became known as the "most dangerous area on the American Continent" and by the end of the century was run by the Gopher Gang (which was very violent) and other gangs. The neighborhood ran from 34th to 59th streets starting west of 8th Avenue to the Hudson River. Oddly enough it was a combination of farmlands and tenements.

If you are looking for a woman with a long career in crime, perhaps Fredericka "Marm" (or "Old Mother") Mandelbaum can serve as a model. She arrived in New York from Prussia with her husband in 1848. They worked as peddlers selling used items and even dressed their horses in trousers to catch attention. The Panic of 1857 was bad for most with more and more hungry children roaming the streets and Marm began organizing and training them in her own Fagin-like operations. In 1865 the Mandelbaums opened a dry goods store as a front and Marm was bankrolling heists, and running gangs of blackmailers, confidence men, and recruiting and training young pickpockets. Her "schools" expanded so that "students" moved from being pickpockets and shoplifters to burglary and safecracking then on to confidence games and blackmail. By 1880 she "was being sought out to fence items by the elite of the light fingered, men like international thief Adam Worth. Because she was now wealthy, she became one of the city's high society hostesses. In 1884 the

Pinkertons infiltrated her organization and arranged a raid on her home. She was arrested, released on bail and fled to Canada with $1 million (the equivalent of nearly $24 million in 2014).

What else can New York City offer us as an urban American Steampunk stage? Corruption via Tammany Hall is probably a given, but we also have public schools coming into existence thanks to residents demands in the 1840s and 1850s. While Marm Mandelbaum was running her school for thieves, the public schools of the Gilded Age could be the perfect place to corrupt young impressionable minds for a villainous inventor type, or for a Steampunk hero or heroine to do the same – not corrupt but build a team of mechanics capable of wondrous things.

There was more than enough violence in the city what with the gang rivalry, and life in general in the tenements being so rough. Tammany Hall officials supplied a lot of Irish with jobs on the police force where they conveniently looked the other way when assigned to a polling location so that ballot boxes could be stuffed. When he was Commissioner of Police in New York City, a young Theodore Roosevelt (in the 1890s) tried to stomp out corruption, prostitutions, and the many other vices that had the city in a tight grip, but the vice lords managed to best him. Roosevelt did arm the New York Police Department in 1896 with Colt New Police Revolvers, a .32 Long Colt caliber, and had his officers trained via pistol practice and qualifying to carry their weapons. Perhaps your Steampunk tinkerer could come up with an even snazzier sidearm...perhaps even some coppers whose sidearm is built into their prosthesis arm if they lost a limb during the war or in action against the gangs. Considering there were frequent complaints of police brutality against immigrants, totally mechanical police with storm trooper programming could be part of a Steampunk New York.

If you are considering a policewoman in your tale, it's a long wait for one to appear historically. There were matrons in the prisons to handle female inmates but no women in uniform on the streets until 1912 when Isabella Goodwin was appointed as the first female detective. Other than female thieves, murderers and prostitutes, the women most likely to spend some time behind bars were suffragettes.

GEARED UP WRITING STEAMPUNK

The Tompkins Square Park Riot of January 13, 1874, is a result of the Panic of 1873 – a depression that lasted several years. Perfect kind of Steampunk opportunity here whether you want to take it in a Luddite direction, a Nativist one, or build a dystopian world as a result of or part of it. The Tompkins Square Park Riot took place in the East Village and matched 1,600 policemen against over 7,000 unemployed workers. Samuel Gompers was there and wrote that "mounted police charged the crowd on Eighth Street, riding them down and attacking men, women, and children without discrimination. It was an orgy of brutality." Amazingly, while there were 46 arrests, no one was killed. In reality, at least. For Steampunk, some innocents would fall if a dystopian angle was taken.

When we think of the makeup of New York City in the mid to later 19th century, it is easy to picture (and hear) a heavily Irish dominated population. What with the Five Points gangs and Tammany Hall angling to get lots of Irishmen on the police force, it simply seems logical. But there was also a large contingent of immigrant citizens (25%) hailing from Germany.

We're going to let the immigrants alone and turn to some awesome structures though.

Did you know that there was a giant reservoir where the New York Public Library stands today on 42nd Street? The Croton Distributing Reservoir and Reservoir Square, built from 1839 to 1842, was a four-acre man-made lake, with a fifty-foot-high, twenty-five-foot-thick granite wall surrounding it. It was a popular promenade for couples and families along the top of the wall. The reservoir was the final link in a system of 41 miles of iron pipe aqueducts that brought fresh water into the city and considered one of the greatest engineering successes of the century. It remained in use until 1900 when it was dismantled, and the library was built. While the city believes it is working quite well through the entire Gilded Age, it seems like an Achilles' heel for the city if a Steampunk villain wishes to get New York under his or her thumb – or an opportunity for an upgrade to something better?

The Brooklyn Bridge is another marvel of the 19th century city. It was completed in 1883 and is the oldest suspension bridge in the U.S., spanning the East River from Manhattan over to Brooklyn (or as the folks in Brooklyn might consider it, going from their shores over to Manhattan). Because of the distance it crossed, the Brooklyn Bridge reigned as the longest suspension bridge in the world until 1903, and it is still the first steel-wire suspension bridge ever built. Are there some Steampunk inventor wheels turning in yon noggins? Should be! Several difficulties arose during the building, one being that workers developed "caisson disease" (similar to the bends that divers fall victim to). The bedrock was further down than expected and the bases of the support towers needed to be sunk 30 foot into that bedrock. The towers themselves are limestone, granite and Rosendale cement, and those granite blocks were sent down from Maine via a schooner. Building it was deadly for some – 27 workmen died over the 13 years it took to build – which isn't a bad number for jobsite related deaths considering what was being accomplished and the length of time construction took – basically 2 deaths a year. That's looking at it statistically, of course, not humanely.

The bridge officially opened May 24, 1883 with bands playing, guns fired from ships and the evening was topped off with a fireworks display. After the big shots got off the bridge, 150,300 people and 1,800 vehicles crossed it the first day. Six days later there was a stampede of people when word was whispered around that the bridge was about to collapse – twelve people were killed, crushed as fellow travelers across the expanse ran over them. The bridge was safe though and to prove it, that master showman P.T. Barnum sent the biggest drawing performer of his circus – Jumbo, the elephant – across it, with another twenty-one elephants trailing along behind their giant leader. Of course, there were jumpers. The first leaped successfully to his death on May 19, 1885. On July 23, 1886, jumper Steve Brodie survived his jump (though some say he didn't jump, just told a tall tale). His name went down in slang history as "taking a Brodie" began to mean taking a chance. Or jumping off a bridge.

Now if you don't need to cross over a bridge, but do need to get around town, you can't take the subway yet. While the Underground was in use in London as early as the 1860s, New York's didn't get rolling until 1904, so you'll need to build one earlier if you want characters to use it. The first elevated railroad, the West Side and Yonkers Patent Railway, was up and running much sooner, between

1867 and 1870 actually. Others followed and soon the elevated tracks made for some very dark, narrow streets. The Galt and Hoy 1879 map of New York City shows not only drawings of buildings packed like sardines along the streets but also the elevated lines.

Grand Central Station opened in 1871, so your characters can catch a train or arrive on one there or can wait until the 20th century for Penn Station to be built. It will take a while considering they plan to tunnel beneath the Hudson River to lay rail and don't break ground for the station itself until 1904, but that doesn't mean you can't build a station of your own to use.

And some notes for time travelers (like ourselves or those in your storylines) here are some tidbits:

- 1876 – The first Telephone Company of New York begins renting telephones to subscribers interested in replacing the telegraphs in businesses

- 1882 – Tom Edison flips on the first electric street lamps in New York

- 1885 - The Museum of Natural History is the tallest building west of Central Park

- 1888 - There is a nasty blizzard in March, so stay in warmer climes

- 1889 - The first Plaza Hotel opens at Central Park South and is "absolutely fireproof"

- 1892 – The first New York to Chicago telephone call is placed

- 1895 – The first New York to San Francisco telephone call is placed

- 1897 - Sunday bicyclers are out in mass, peddling near the now completed Grant's Tomb on Riverside Drive

New York City offers every type of Steampunk character opportunities except any looking to manufacture items in great quantities. That takes space and the Island of Manhattan simply doesn't have it to spare — historically, that is. It's always possible to carve out a mechanical or scientific kingdom here. All it takes is some heartless removal of tenements, a bit of digging of underground tunnels and caverns prior to the subways and deeper than the sewers. For a Steampunk author, New York City can merely sit on the top of a wondrous iceberg of invention.

Go forth and dream it up.

La Belle Époch
1871 – 1914

Where Britain has both the Victorian and Edwardian eras and the U.S. has the Gilded Age, Europe has La Belle Époch. Yes, it's French, though it tends to be the term used for more than one Continental European country during this period. The era covers 1871 through 1914, which makes it perfect for our purposes. We'll cover more than merely what is happening in Paris though and head East to see how the German principalities are advancing, too.

France
The French of the upper and middle class were doing very well from the close of the Franco-Prussian War to the start of World War I, which is why these years were called "The Beautiful Age". The Industrial Revolution's glories had trickled out of Britain and into the mainstream of West and Central Europe. Politically things were fairly peaceful and calm in France (except for ruckuses by anarchists, monarchists, republicans and nationalists) and they were doing a bit of empire building by staking claims in in 3rd world locales. In 1830 they'd attached Algiers. By 1900, the French flag waved over possessions in North, West, and Central Africa, covering parts of the Congo, Somaliland, Senegal, the Ivory Coast, Mali, and Guinea. From 1861 to 1867 the French were attempting to run or influence things in Mexico. From 1867 through 1887 French Indochina (Cambodia, parts of modern Viet Nam) fell into their hands. Holdings in China came through leases, the first granted in 1849 in Shanghai, which lasted through the close of World War II. In 1880, Tahiti was annexed.

Militarily, things are quiet for France once the Franco-Prussian war ends in 1871. General Georges Boulanger becomes Minister of War and reorganizes things, but while we may not have heard of him, Alfred Dreyfus could well ring a bell. The Dreyfus Affair occurred in 1894 when Captain Dreyfus was accused and convicted of selling military secrets to the Germans. Sentenced to exile on Devil's Island (an appropriately named rocky isle in shark infested waters in the

Atlantic), Dreyfus was pulled from the penal colony for a retrial that exonerated him. He'd already spent nearly five years on Devil's Island for a crime that investigative journalists proved had been committed by another man on the same military staff.

The French Foreign Legion came into being in 1831, so it is well established by the Belle Époch. Oddly enough, it is an organization that tends to have only 25% of the members hailing from France. It was the perfect place to disappear for men who had a reason for wanting to disappear. Even Frenchmen who wanted to had a way to do so – they claimed they were from Belgium. The officers were always Frenchmen, but the men of a station might come from anywhere in Europe. There were even some Americans who joined. It was originally formed to clear out troublemakers and set them to fighting where it served the good of the Empire, particularly the French colonies of Africa. However, during the Belle Époch men of the French Foreign Legion served in the Torkin campaign (China) and the Sino-French war of 1883-1888 as well. They were in the field in Africa for the second Franco-Dahomean War of 1892-1894, the second Madagascar Expedition in 1894-1895, and the Mandingo War of 1898. If you'd like to work in a war but not one that is all that familiar to readers, choosing one where your characters end up as members of the French Foreign Legion might offer some interesting possibilities. Just supply them with some helpful Steampunk technology.

Not surprising to have it said that La Belle Époch was the first era to feel the full impact of the modern world. Not only had investigative journalism come into being, but technology made the relaying of news around the world seem to take place in the blink of an eye...well, compared to waiting for details to be delivered by post or prior systems which were rather Jurassic compared to telegraphs, international cable systems, and telephones, that is.

In a Steampunk world either the transmission of news can be still further enhanced, or prisoners headed to Devil's Island be delivered to their exile via an airship. Perhaps they could plot a way to take the ship over or build one of their own!

Things for the most part were very good in France. New technology allowed goods to get to markets faster as railways spread out across the landscape. Industry grew and was in place when demands arrived for automobiles then flying machines in the new century. Of course, there were bicycles – there were 375,000 being ridden in 1898 and 3.5 million French men, women, and children were peddling to and fro by 1914. The first Tour de France takes place in 1903. Because it was possible to get places easier – either via bicycle, train, or, as the century turned, automobile, more people became interested in sports (as spectators as well as players) and in taking holidays. With wages on the rise, and the life expectancy of children, life was indeed beautiful.

This period might say "art" to you for Toulouse-Lautrec, Tissot, Picasso, Renoir and others are hanging out in the Montmartre area of Paris. The Folies Bergère changes to a music hall venue in 1886, although it has been around for a few decades already. The Moulin Rouge flung open its doors in 1889. The painters (and other clientele) might have come to watch the scandalous can-can performed by the dancers at music halls. The can-can had originated as a variation on the gallop, a couples dance, in 1830 – all the young people were dancing it as it upped the ante on athleticism as well as was frowned on by their parents. By the 1890s it had become a choreographed dance performed by women on stage and involved a lot of skirt shaking and high kicks by black stockinged legs. A dancer would bet a man she could take his hat off without using her hands, then kick it off. A kick might also serve as a warning regarding unwanted advances. Can't you see a Steampunk heroine delivering can-can kicks in place of martial art ones when in a tight spot in Paris?

Heroines will be able to purchase ready-made suits (jacket and skirt ensembles) beginning in the 1880s. Jackets alone had been available for a decade but expected to merely top off a bustled skirt a woman already owned. Bicycling outfits might suit a heroine but after 1900 she will no doubt require a motoring outfit when driving in an automobile. If she is of the upper crust and needs a ball gown, the House of Worth is turning out stunning creations. But so are Doucet and Poiret. Jeanne Paquin is perhaps one of the first female designers, and she's moving closets away from the gowns of the past into 20th century fare. In 1913 a fresh young thing, Coco Chanel, opens her first boutique, selling deluxe casual apparel, using menswear fabrics and looser fits.

Perhaps the most famous element of La Belle Épach in Paris is the building of the Eifel Tower for the 1889 international fair. Prior to that, Eifel had been busy building bridges and viaducts. His 984-foot tower took two years to build. It was still the marvel that drew people to the 1900 World's Fair. This is also the fair to make excellent use of electricity, lighting the grounds so that visitors lingered into the evening to enjoy the illuminated fountains, if not the many exhibits featuring the latest marvels of the Industrial world, one of which was the moving walkway, the "street of the future"! Electricity also ran the trams of the metro line.

The first moving picture was shown in Paris by the Lumière Brothers on December 28, 1895. By 1900 going to the movies was a popular pastime. Between the start of the new century and 1913 there were over a hundred theatres showing moving pictures – silent, of course, but marvelous in their own right. No reason a Steampunk character of yours can't do a bit of modification or even open the first multiplex!

Handy to know for characters looking for housing, demolition of whole neighborhoods had occurred during the 1850s and 1860 as Paris began taking on the contours visitors associate with it today. Things like piped in drinking water (the Seine was only good for fountains and street cleaning), drainage sewers, and the construction of tunnels that later housed telegraph and telephone lines, pneumatic mail tubes and electric wiring for homes, thus making the use of utility poles unnecessary, are all in place. All the improvements weren't below ground for some old streets were eliminated with three times as many new ones replacing them, then sidewalks were laid – over 700 miles worth – and trees planted along the new byways. And it all happened in basically twenty years' time with no new taxes imposed!

The old upper class, *le gratin*, tended to live in the quiet Faubourg Saint-Germain area although the premier address was the Champs-Elysées. Entertaining among the wealthy was frequent and lavish. There are still Paris salons where the well-connected hostesses hobnob on a weekly basis with artists, writers, actors, composers, politicians — the famous and the (within reason) infamous. The Belle Époch is probably the last era for the salon though. In a Steampunk world, surely there will be a few engineers and scientists included. In fact, M. Eifel probably received an invite or two once his tower was receiving rave reviews.

The Seine at the turn of the century was crowded with fishing vessels, barges, and *bateaux-mouches*, which served rather like river taxis handy for both local workers and visitors in getting from one side of the river to the other. The *Métro* wasn't up and running as quickly as the Underground in London, but it was in use by the late 1890s, which allows it to beat out New York's subway system which didn't go into action until the 20th century. A further note about the *Métropolitain* revolves around the entrances to the system, which featured *art nouveau* cast iron work, which was considered controversial and daring. The entrances featured electric lighting in the iron flowers and glass roofs. Fortunately, the public loved the look.

Everything changes in 1914 when war breaks out, but while the Edwardian period covers the war years, La Belle Époch does not. That doesn't mean you can't set a Steampunk story in France during the war. It merely means, information about it won't be found here. Instead we head to...

Germany

Considering that Germany will have such a large presence in the coming war (WW I), it is downright sluggish when it comes to taking advantage of the technology pioneered in Britain. But until 1871, Germany is a conglomeration of small principalities each with their own rulers. Those that could, built rail lines, though they tended to be webs spread out from market towns. Canals had been built to augment getting goods to the major rivers, like the Danube, with steamboats plying the waterways. Travel between principalities facilitated growth, many borders were being crossed en route to prosperity. Still, some of the *Zollverein* (the 25 separate states) were so small that shipped goods needed to be unloaded and reloaded for customs officials two or three times a day in some cases.

Prussia had the most extensive network and had benefited from its rails during the Seven Weeks War of 1866 and the Franco-Prussian War of 1870, moving troops and supplies into place quickly. Something else Prussia had was Otto von Bismarck. He was instrumental in the creation of the German Empire, which combined those 25 separate "countries" into one in 1871.

It was only in the 19th century that the commonalities of the German states began being emphasized, and it was an offshoot of the ease, speed and a reduction in the price of travel made possible by improved roads, the canals and the railroad. Jakob and Wilhelm Grimm did more than collect folk tales, they compiled what became known as *The Grimm*, a massive dictionary of the German language as spoken throughout the Zollverein. And with travel made easier, Karl Baedeker began writing travel guides about various Central European cities and regions. He supplied details on distances, hiking paths, roads to avoid, places to stay and in listings things to see gave brief histories of famous buildings, castles, battlefields and famous people that might be of interest. A Steampunk character could benefit from one of Baedeker's books, wouldn't you think? They might go down one of those roads that he recommended not using, curious about why he warned visitors away from those paths.

Most of the railways (90%) were in place by 1880, and with all those border stops no longer necessary, things moved along swiftly now.

Once they were all under one heading, The German Empire (1871-1918), there was something other than transportation and improved markets that people wanted: more territory. Why should everyone else have colonies and not the Germans, right? Bismarck was hesitant but gave way to popular opinion (and maybe some prods from Kaiser Wilhelm I, his boss) in 1880. In quick succession Togo and property in the Cameroons, and south-west and east Africa were acquired. New Guinea, the Marshall Islands and the Bismarck Archipelago were snapped up in Oceania.

There are scientists and inventors busy in Germany during the Belle Époch that might be helpful to know about in concocting a Steampunk tale. Heinrich Anton de Bary coins the word *symbiosis* in 1879. He's the Father of Phytopathology, the science of plant diseases and modern mycology. The electric incandescent lamp is invented in 1882. Emil Adolph von Behring discovers the diphtheria antitoxin in 1891, which is the first cure of a disease. Other creations are: Benz's gasoline powered automobile, Diesel's engine, the Bunsen burner, the electric incandescent lamp, the electricity driven hand drill, echo sounding, the C.R.T. oscilloscope, Telemobiskop (precursor of radio), and of course Ferdinand Graf von Zepplin has his giant flying cigar. Germany was in the forefront in chemistry and was the premier European steel-producing nation by the close of the 19th century, too. The new century gets kicked off by young Albert Einstein's theory of relativity being formulated ($E=mc^2$).

Few people have telephones, though the first telephone exchange opens in Berlin in January 1881. By 1900 people still prefer to send letters or telegraphs but this is because having a telephone is an expensive proposition. The further one lives from the exchange, the more it costs. Still enough telephones are hooked up to result in the first directory to be published in July. The world's first electric tram line opens near Berlin in 1881 as well.

In 1888 there is some Kaiser shifting as Wilhelm I dies, is succeeded by his son Frederick III who dies of throat cancer three months later and thus the crown goes to Wilhelm II, who is 29 years old. The new Kaiser dislikes Bismarck's conservative outlook – he wants to turn the German Empire into one as vast as Victoria's – vaster, if possible. Bismarck is out of a job in 1890. First step on this path is to build a bigger and better navy. 1898 sees major warship building, but it also sees more colony grabbing as Germany acquires footholds in China and snags the Marianas, the Caroline Islands and Samoa, which has teeth grinding in Britain, the U.S., Russia and Japan. German banks finance the building of the Baghdad Railway which links the German Empire to that of the Turks and locations in the Persian Gulf.

If you are thinking of using Bismarck himself as a character – even one seen from a distance – it might be handy to know that he smoked fourteen cigars every day and until 1884 he drank beer during the day, wines at dinner and a whole bottle of champagne before he headed to bed because it helped him sleep. Apparently, his doctor strongly suggested that he not drink quite so much.

Germany was jockeying into position for what would come in 1914 when Serbian assassins take out the Austrian Archduke Ferdinand, and all the various treaties made between nations kick in to create World War I, the war to end all wars, the war that spells the close of La Belle Époch, the Beautiful Era.

Other Worlds

We've talked about changing the world that was here on Earth, but in Steampunk it is also possible to journey to worlds that aren't — well, that we don't know for sure whether they do exist. These are the parallel worlds and alternative universes.

Scientific theorists say there is a possibility that such places exist but until someone can journey to one and return to tell about it, these are the realms of fiction writers alone.

So, what's the difference between the two?

The Parallel World

The *fictional* difference is that in a parallel world characters enter a world that is another Earth with very little of it changed — except in our case, this parallel world has evolved with Steampunk elements while ours has not, and it still *is* a Steampunk era similar to our various late 19th century and early 20th century periods.

A character can go from the 19th century world they know into this Steampunk parallel world or they could be quite happy living in the 21st century and somehow stumble into this parallel world. They could stumble into it from further in the future or father back in the past, too. Not too far back in the past but there are historical personages who would feel right at home in a Steampunk world because the Renaissance one they lived in made what they were interested in rather dangerous considering it could turn the eye of the Inquisition on them. Leonardo Da Vinci and Galileo Galilei might be stunned at first, but they'd adapt.

This parallel world will have the same 19th century costuming, the attitudes of society are likely similar, and the same progress (though with Steampunk tweaks). Many of the same personages could turn up but there can be differences — in fact, there *should* be differences. While this is a parallel world it isn't a carbon copy one. It should remain recognizably a Victorian or American West or Belle Époch community or whatever other niche you'd like to pluck from our world and plop down in this parallel one. This is the world where several "what ifs" have actually occurred in history and set it on a different course, maybe for centuries!

The Alternative Universe

The *fictional* alternative universe has only one thing in common with our *actual* universe – it has a planet that is similar to Earth in atmosphere, is populated by beings who while they might not all look like *homo sapiens* will live in a civilization that is very like that of the Victorian, Edwardian, Old American West, Urban Eastern, rural or urban colonies of Empires, or the Belle Époch. It will have Steampunk machinery, created beings (perhaps some of those citizens are the result of odd matings or gene splicing), dystopian areas as well as a section of society that is the wealthy elite. There will be police forces, military forces, merchants, artists, politicians…the works. The system they work under might be very altered from any found-on Earth proper or a parallel Earth though. This is not the planet Earth. The worlds and stars visible in the night sky are not those of our own universe. This universe can be built from scratch to your own specifications. Perhaps their religion honors the Great Mechanic, the Architect of Life and those who are this god's chosen have built everything on this world.

The Alternative Steampunk Universe story can be peopled only by characters from this world and their difficulties. It doesn't require that Earthlings show up for difficulties to arise and need to be dwelt with. The people may look different, but they do live in a knockoff of the 19th century we're familiar with. China Miéville's *Perdito Street Station* takes place in such a world.

But Earthlings can stumble into this one as easily as they do the Parallel World. It's simply that the Alternative Universe isn't exactly Earth in another dimension. It's merely Earth-like in many aspects (like oxygen atmosphere, gravity level, carbon-based life forms for the most part, rock based surface, and sufficient water). And it evolved into being a Steampunk type world, of course.

How Do You Get There?

Of course, one of the things you'll need to decide is how your characters get to either the parallel world or into an alternative universe if they are Earthlings.

If they are from way, *way* into the future and in space, a wormhole or blackhole can be the answer, but it they are 19th century or earlier Earthlings, then another direction will need to be taken unless you invent a way for them to be en route to Mars, of course.

We can take a leaf from the Time Travel handbook in this case because if a machine or time warp or displacement in the fabric of time that creates a shimmering veil or a fog or a visual displacement or an entry way simply opens up suddenly before a character for time travel, it can all work as a way to travel to a world of your own making.

A modern scientist might be involved in a freak accident in their lab that sends them hurtling into this other world.

Remember, you don't necessarily *need* a visitor from Earth in the Alternative Universe, and the same probably holds true of the Parallel World, but if at least one of your major characters *is* an Earthling, the set up for their arrival in the parallel world or alternative universe will need to be laid out so that there is a certain logic to it. *Certain* being the pertinent word here for if you have a scientist whose lab accident is letting matter and anti-matter particles get too close to each other, well, there goes reality for everyone else, right? But if he or she was at ground zero for the annihilation of our own universe, perhaps this lone survivor ended up in that new dimension.

Should you decide to send a character so far off planet that they're out of this universe entirely, do put a lot of thought into how the journey was accomplished. There is nothing that can turn a reader away faster than for a writer to use a scenario that the reader might know is absolute rubbish. This might be fiction, but it does need to follow some rules. Consider this one that shouldn't be broken.

CREATE A MACHINE

We already built a created being but what we also need to do is build some machinery!

This can use clockwork technology or be powered by steam, or a combination of both. What it needs to do is be our graphic Steampunk element...though of course, we'll be painting it with words, not pictures. Okay, there might be pictures on the cover but that comes long after the mental construction of these elements.

So, what can they be? Likely a lot of gears, things that the reader can mentally see turning, one into the other, driving this creation to *do* something.

Can it be a biological? Well, in the case of Westerfeld's Darwinian creations there might be an argument that it can be, but "machine" doesn't say biological to me...and probably not to most readers either. We'll leave that element back in the "Create A Being" category.

This means we're using iron, steel, copper, brass and any new mixture you might invent to pour into molds, beat with a blacksmith's hammer, file down, curl into a spring, and whatever other process seems appropriate or that you've invented.

However, it also will likely require lubricants, fuels, or in the case of a meld between something biological (but not sentient) and a metallic, a formula. That and an operation to insert a controlling unit might turn a man or beast into a machine though. Key element would be it now no longer thinks or acts without being programmed to do something.

Things to take into consideration are size as well as materials. And purpose.

While Josephine Cochran not only invented the first dishwasher (for use in restaurants), she was granted a patent on it in late December 1886, the first popup toaster doesn't turn up until 1919. I hope everyone knows that typewriters, cash registers and sewing machines arrived much earlier, but that's in *real* history. Wouldn't a Steampunk inventor husband or brother or beau consider being the first man to get on a woman's nerves by giving her an *appliance* for a gift? One he created just for her? Or the modern minded Steampunk heroine eases her own life by inventing something to give her more time to draw up new schematics. What about a garbage disposer that isn't a pig in the backyard?

There is hot and cold water available at homes in cities but what about out on the prairie? An inventor drifting into a rail or mining town could become quite popular by supplying such a convenience. What about a clothes dryer that doesn't involve a rope attached to posts and pins to hold clothing, sheets, towels, tablecloths, etc., to it while the breeze takes its good old time drying them?

Granted, these aren't usually the types of machines that come to mind when building a Steampunk backdrop or world, but they are very viable ones.

We tend to think more of those Difference Engines, the things with massive wheels, cogs, gears, pistols...big backdrop items.

Or transportation: trains, dirigibles, horseless carriages, diesel powered motorcycles, early flying machines, or as Artemis Gordon uses in the movie *Wild, Wild West*, a rocket propelled penny-farthing style of bicycle. I suppose we shouldn't forget Dr. Loveless's giant mechanical spider either though. But why not a transpositional displacement enciphlercator. And, yes, I made that one up. However, if you've got one, you could say, "Beam me up, Scotty."

Or communication: telegraph, pneumatic tube, mechanical passenger pigeon, trans-oceanic cables, radio waves, the telephone, or some upgraded version of some of these. Or at least a more convoluted looking one.

But the first thing that might come to many minds is weapons.

While earlier in the era the pistols and rifles were still one shot wonders – and the enemy could take you out with a shot while you reloaded, which is never good for morale – by mid-century improvements were coming fast on the heels of each other.

Multi-shot guns began to be produced, and in all sizes and configurations, but sometimes it was distance that was the #1 item on a shooter's list of requirements. Well, it might have duked it out with *accuracy* when hitting the target. The weapon that provided both was a single shot rifle though. The Sharps. I'll reference a movie that is *not* a Steampunk one here as a visual aid, and in it Mathew Quigley (aka Tom Selleck) can hit a target a really, really long distance away. He uses a Sharps rifle in *Quigley Down Under*. While this was still a single shot rifle, it was the perfect weapon for a sharpshooter to pick off a target at a great distance as well as quickly reload thanks to breech loading, easy for a kneeling man to accomplish. If the fella – or thing – you were targeting didn't have one as well, you were pretty safe. Wouldn't it be handy for your inventor to figure out a way to make it also capable of more than a single shot before a reload was necessary though? And it doesn't necessarily need to be the good guy who does it.

The Sharps isn't the kind of weapon that can mow the enemy down, though. However, the first rapid fire repeating weapon that can is the Gatling gun, which arrived in the 1860s. It was used during the American Civil War and a lot of wars after that, in various parts of the world, too. Want to consider making a gunner obsolete once it's set in action? I'll bet a villain would. Makes it so much easier to take over the world after making the populace cower before such a weapon, doesn't it?

But if you're thinking Weird West style Steampunk, you're thinking fellas wearing six-guns on their belt. That is, pistols capable of firing six shoots before needing a reload. That was deadly progress. In my own Steampunk world, my "Q" built attachments to reduce the kick of a gun (something I discovered exists today) and gave it a self-targeting system for shooters who weren't sharpshooters to begin with. It could improve their aim.

Yes, there are cannon, and rockets (which were used by Wellington's troops during the Napoleonic Wars, though maybe not as successfully as later). There were bombs, and chances are someone had figured out how to set a timer with a clockwork to set it off. If they hadn't, well, your characters could or could upgrade one that actually existed.

We could talk armor, not the medieval type, but something capable of stopping a bullet (ref: *Wild, Wild West* again), or even mechanized blow guns with poisoned or at least incapacitating drugs in the dart's point.

GEARED UP WRITING STEAMPUNK

However, we could get off weapons and other inventions entirely and move on to what to call things! That's always fun. Suffice to say that when it comes to "decorating" your Steampunk set and supplying items characters will use, think over the top or upgrade or simply invent something before its time.

GEARED UP WRITING STEAMPUNK

Period Jargon plus Naming People and Things

Remember that transpositional displacement enciphlercator? Well, I think the one thing that you can say across the board is that the 19th century liked big convoluted words (even the fairly uneducated) and that in Steampunk you can take that and run with it. (For machines ref: the far too short-lived show *Legend* as well as *Wild, Wild West*.)

I wouldn't use it for everything. Because you'll have characters who aren't inventors or scientists going "Huh?" My Covert Cogs have Galileans they use – an upgrade on binoculars, so not all items need to have long, tongue-twisting names. But a few of them could.

There are lots of different ways characters can speak in a Steampunk novel. In England, they could drop words only found in dictionaries…or thesauruses…or use "vulgar" language, that is thieves cant or Cockney rhyming slang or words that are distinctly Irish or Welsh or Scottish or borrowed from time spent in India. They could be scientific words. While Deanna Raybourn's Veronica Speedwell books aren't Steampunk, they do take place in 1890s England and Veronica frequently kills time by mentally cataloging the various species of butterflies she has captured in her net on previous trips to distant locations around the world. She uses both their common name and the science bound Latin one. In Sabrina Flynn's Ravenwood Mysteries, set in turn of the century San Francisco (also not Steampunk), even Chinese words get used when a case takes A.J. or Bel to Chinatown locations. You don't have to invent words for your Steampunk story because the period itself supplies a great selection to flavor your story stew.

There is a section in Mark Twain's *Roughing It* where he gives a dialog between an educated minister and a miner attempting to arrange a friend's funeral. The miner's speech is laden with sports terms while the minister's is littered with those from a different stratum of the education ladder. It's a difficult meeting of minds as neither is quite following what the other is saying, yet they finally settle the problem. It's a very funny section and Twain at his rollicking best. It's worth looking up to use as a model.

With so many immigrants in all the large cities, there will be lots of words used that others might not understand and yet will get the gist of in a conversation.

Plus, insults. A story set in the American West within a few years of the War Between the States (which went by many names, depending upon which side you were on), the degrading terms hurled by Union soldiers at the Confederate brothers and vice versa definitely give a firm period "sound" to a story.

There are lots of period series on cable TV that can supply the "sound" for you, too, but my personal favorite is *The Great Train Robbery*, the movie version of Michael Crichton's novel of the same way. Donald Sutherland's thief slang is wonderful to hear, and if I want to use the police in a Victorian setting, I'll definitely want some character to call them *The Crushers*. Of course, any immigrant from Victoria's kingdom who arrives in America or Canada or Australia might call them that no matter what land they've arrived in. It is worth remembering that the Australians have plenty of slang of their own, too.

Names of characters can be convoluted or ordinary, as well. Among my Covert Cogs I have Langston Avery, but I also have Mick Tindale. Samanthalia Gast has a sister Cog named Ariel Knapp, but another is Zephyr McCabe. And on an undercover assignment, Mena Katchem goes by Professor Ethelmena von Katchemstross, a name Heath Haymes sneers at in disbelief. In the first Steampunk story I ever wrote, which was a Victorian, my heroine's name was Pesperone Bashlingburg and I went all out on giving nearly everyone in the cast at least of something strange in their name. They were high middle-class society folk, so it seemed quite proper to do so. If you do use these sorts of names, reserve them for comedic elements. In this I'm sort of following P.G. Wodehouse's lead – and while he passed away before Steampunk was a thing, he lived in the era when Verne, Wells, Doyle and others were writing, so he is a "period" piece himself, and had many, many characters with ridiculous names.

GEARED UP WRITING STEAMPUNK

The best thing to do is counter the absurd names with far more common ones usually. Though I will admit that my Archedelphos Fizwick, Esquire, isn't exactly from around these parts.

The Final Product

Steampunk is one of the most exciting, frustrating, thrilling, and fascinating genres available to a writer. It offers so many ways to combine elements from other genres and genre niches. Ways to change history to our own liking, not that we'd want to live in these worlds ourselves, usually.

The Industrial Revolution might have begun in Britain, but by mid-century it had spread out to all areas of the world, largely, in part, due to the colonization of third world areas by the various Empires, some small, some large. It brought about the era of imagination in science as well as machine works. Competition kept everyone primed for new discoveries, new products.

Now it is our turn to turn out new products – new stories of what might have been happening in a different realm, on a different world, in a parallel or alternative universe, if only one thing was changed – or more than one.

So go forth and spin your tale. Once it's finished and polished to a high sheen, set it free to fly onto the desk of an editor at one of the publishing houses listed on the following pages.

GEARED UP WRITING STEAMPUNK

The Marketplace

Once you've done your research, tweaked your history, mixed and matched elements and characters and come up with a plot, it's time to figure out where to send your completed manuscript.

That's what this section is all about. It would be terribly remiss not to mention where you could find editors interested in reading Steampunk manuscripts, wouldn't it?

Never fear. Such was never going to be the case. Because Steampunk is a subdivision of fantasy, fantasy publishers are listed here even though they may not have had a Steampunk title released...yet. I did try to point out which ones *did* mention it or had a title showing in their current catalog that leaned toward Steam. But I still suggest you check the online catalogues for each to keep abreast of what they are releasing. Also keep an eye peeled for editors' announcements in blogs and tweets as they will frequently leak the word "Steampunk" when looking for new submissions.

One caution: some publishers will not look at even a query letter much less a manuscript submission without it having an agent attached to it. I indicated when such was the case, though most of the publishers in this new and improved – and packed! – list seemed open to submissions sans agents. Others will take a query letter but not a proposal without a request to see it. And then there are the third type, the ones who will not only look at an unagented submission package but prefer to see the entire manuscript. As there are always changes in submission policies, check the publisher-in question's website for an update on what they are looking for and how they want to see it. And, just because it's listed doesn't mean I recommend it because, frankly, many of these publishers are new to me. You should be the best judge of what meets your wish list regarding publication. These are listed in alphabetical order, rather than be ranked on desirability – just so you know.

GEARED UP WRITING STEAMPUNK

ACE/ROC
Berkley/Penguin Group Publishing
Agented and unagented accepted
www.penguingroup.com
Manuscript guidelines online via FAQ
Looking for 80,000 to 125,000 words
Query e-mail **sff@us.penguingroup.com**
Check the guidelines first though

AETHON BOOKS
Standalone or series potential fantasy
Alternative History noted which implies
Steampunk to me without saying it
They like time travel, too.
Will look at 60,000 and up words but prefer 80,000 word ms.
No advance, but those are scarce these days anyway
www.aethonbooks.com/submissions

ANGRY ROBOT BOOKS
UK based publisher that does give advances
However, an agent is required to get in the door usually
But they do have a specific open to submissions period every year
when unagented manuscripts can get in the door
Check the website for when the notice goes up
Their latest list of published books does have
a Steampunk title in the lineup though
https://www.angryrobotbooks.com/submissions/

ANTARCTIC PRESS
Comic book press but they required an author to
do it all – storyline and artwork – Magma/Anime style preferred
http://www.antarctic-press.com/html/submissions.php

AVON IMPULSE
E-book division for Avon romance at HarperCollins
Also the only way Avon accepts submissions

GEARED UP WRITING STEAMPUNK

without an agent now
www.avonimpulse.com
Submission guidelines online
But Steampunk is noted as a genre of interest,
Must be romance though

BAEN BOOKS
Sci-fi and fantasy publisher
Steampunk not specifically mentioned but
They do have alternative history books published
No agent requirement listed
They don't want to see query letters, won't open them
100,000 – 130,000 words required
Reports in 9 to 12 months
www.baen.com

BELLE BOOKS
Publishes fantasy and YA.
50K and up word count
http://www.bellebooks.com/shopcontent.asp?type=For%20Writers
Offers advance
One year to publication
Possibility of e-book, print, and audio

BURNS AND LEA BOOKS
A new publishing house that kicked off with
both Gaslamp Holmesian fantasy and urban fantasy titles in 2019
They are also open to Steampunk (I asked)
They prefer novels between 85,000 and 90,000 words
https://www.burnsandleabooks.com/submissions

CARINA PRESS
Division of Harlequin – E-books only
www.CarinaPress.com
Lists Steampunk as something they are looking for
See website for guidelines
Agented or unagented submissions

GEARED UP WRITING STEAMPUNK

Submissions via Electronic only

CHANDRA PRESS
Only open to submissions in August
Basically a sci-fi publisher but if you write stories that combine space and Steampunk, say like *Firefly*, they might be interested
No word counts given or much of anything else on their website but might be worth a shot
www.https://www.chandrapress.com/submission

CHAMPAGNE BOOKS
Steampunk is no longer listed specifically, though fantasy is mentioned
40,000-130,000 words
http://champagnebooks.com/store/content/2-submissions#OtherGenres
No simultaneous submissions

CHEEKY FRAWG EDICIONES NEVSKY
Speak and write Spanish? Unfortunately, I don't so all I'm going on here is that this publisher released a BEST OF SPANISH STEAMPUNK book in English
https://edicionesnevsky.com/

DAW BOOKS, INC./PENGUIN PUTNAM
https://www.penguin.com/publishers/daw/
Agented and unagented submissions accepted
Manuscript guidelines online
Advance against royalties, 3 months to hear back

DEL REY/BALLANTINE BOOKS
DEL REY/SPECTRA
A division of Random House. Agent required.
www.penguinrandomhouse.com/

GEARED UP WRITING STEAMPUNK

Manuscript guidelines online
Advance against royalties

DIVERTIR PRESS
Looks like they are fairly new, books listed all released in 2019
They don't mention Steampunk by name but do note
fantasy and alternative history is of interest
60,000 – 80,000 words, no mention of agent
http://divertirpublishing.com/forauthors.html

EDGE SCIENCE FICTION AND FANTASY PUBLISHING
TESSERACT BOOKS
Canadian publisher
Actually prefers unagented manuscript proposals
www.edgewebsite.com
Manuscript guidelines online
75,000 to 100,000 words
No simultaneous submissions
A bit confusing since in one spot they say
only snail mail paper submission
yet at another they give an electronic submission address
e-mail to michelle@hadespublications.com
electronic submissions in WORD only, no pdfs
Advance against royalties; reports in 3 to 4 months
Query only if you are unsure whether your ms. suits them
Publishes 18-20 months after acceptance

ENTANGLED PUBLISHING
Basically, a romance publisher, so that's a required element
Accepts unagented submissions
www.entangledpublishing.com
Novels 70,000 to 120,000 words
Novellas 20,000 to 40,000 words
Manuscript guidelines online
Electronic submission only

EXCALIBUR BOOKS

GEARED UP WRITING STEAMPUNK

Publishes fantasy and I saw a Steampunk cover in the book catalog
Based in Tokyo but publishing in English, too
They don't appear to have a website with their name on it
So here is what there is: http://johnpaulcatton.com/
They also have Twitter (@ExcaliburBooks) and an email (ExcaliburBooks@gmail.com)
They do prefer settings in Japan, though

EXCESSION PRESS

Their website says they do "weird western"
To me, this equates to Weird West Steampunk
They may have another concept, like *Cowboys and Aliens*
However, they mention that they like
William Gibson and China Miéville, both Steam authors
Check with them first, in other words
They offer a $300 advance and want fairly short ms.
30,000 to 60,000 words
Unlike nearly everyone else, they aren't interested in series books
https://www.excessionpress.com/p/submissions.html

FLAME TREE PRESS

Fantasy is one of the interests their website notes,
but it doesn't go into specific niches
They have a lot of short story collections and
among them was one called *Shorts and Steam*.
There was also a collection mentioning
Queen Victoria's reign as the link tying it together
Otherwise they have H.G. Wells and Conan Doyle collections
70,000 to 120,000 preferred word count
https://www.flametreepress.com/submissions/
I really included them because they were a publisher
willing to look at previously published works,
either self-published/Indie or traditionally published,
though I'm guessing they'll want to see sales reports
Worth noting though

GREY GECKO PRESS

GEARED UP WRITING STEAMPUNK

Listed for fantasy in *Writer's Digest Novel and Short Story Markets 2020*
but they haven't posted on their blog since 2015
Novellas to novels so word count is 25,000 to 175,000
Currently showing closed to submissions because they're swapped
They even note how many are still being read. It was 567 when I pulled them up
http://greygeckopress.com/submissions/

HADLEY RILLE BOOKS
Agented and unagented queries accepted by email
https://hadleyrillebks.wordpress.com/contact-us/submission-guidelines/
Guidelines on website
Advance against royalties;
Publication generally 6 months after acceptance

HYRA PUBLICATIONS
Accepts unagented manuscripts
Electronic with some trade paper releases
https://hydrapublications.com/submissions/
70,000 to 100,00 words desired length
Steampunk was specifically mentioned as part of the fantasy genre niches of interest

JO FLETCHER BOOKS
UK firm, Imprint of Quercus which is part of Hachette UK
Fantasy and horror publisher though Steampunk not specified
But they say "novels right across the fantastical spectrum"
They publish Clive Barker and Eoin Colfer, so big names
Do take unsolicited submissions, see guidelines.
Reports in 6 months
https://www.jofletcherbooks.com/landing-page/jo-fletcher-books/jo-fletcher-books-submissions/

INKITT PUBLISHING
Not so much a publisher as a place to post novels

GEARED UP WRITING STEAMPUNK

As they say, it's "Reader Powered"
Not sure what that equates to but
if you're looking for exposure to your fiction
possibly worth a look
https://www.inkitt.com/guidelines

INSPIRED QUILL
Another UK publisher with a listed interest in Steampunk
55,000 to 120,00 words
No mention an agent required
https://www.inspired-quill.com/submissions/

KENSINGTON PUBLISHING CORP.
Not a fantasy publisher but has
2 editors noting an interest in sci/fi/fantasy
Conflicted listing as it says agent required
but also that unagented manuscripts are accepted
www.kensingtonbooks.com
Check website for submission policies
Accepts simultaneous submissions
Advance against royalties
Publishes 12 to 24 months after acceptance

NIGHTSCAPE PRESS
More a horror press, but maybe your Steam tale
leans to horror! It's why I've included them
They do calls for submissions so check the submissions page
Short stories, novelettes, and novellas: 15,000 to 50,000 words
maybe
http://www.nightscapepress.pub/p/submissions.html

PHANTASM BOOKS
Steampunk 85,000 to 125,000 words
http://www.assentpublishing.com/Submissions.aspx
no mention of agent required

THE PARLIAMENT HOUSE PUBLISHERS

GEARED UP WRITING STEAMPUNK

Sci-Fantasy publisher with a few other things tossed in
One editor did mention Steampunk as an interest
No mention of agents, 50,000 to 140,000 words
http://www.parliamenthousepress.com/submissions
they do accept previously published – even self-published/Indie -- manuscripts

PARVUS PRESS
Speculative fantasy publisher with at least one Steampunk title
Check to see whether they are currently open for submissions though as they have certain submission periods
No mention of agent or word count
Does pay an advance (average is $500) against royalties
https://parvuspress.com/submissions/

RED ADEPT PUBLISHING
Publishes fantasy of 50,000+ words
YA and over 18 audiences
Submission electronically via their online form
http://redadeptpublishing.com/submissions/

ROSARIUM PUBLISHING
A mention of Steampunk being among the fantasy genres
Of interest to them but no word count was given
No mention that an agent is required
No submission guidelines available
http://rosariumpublishing.com/index.html

STEAMPUNK MAGAZINE
Not a paying market and allows noncommercial reproduction of stories published in it
But if you're looking for a start for your publishing vita, worth considering
http://www.steampunkmagazine.com/deadlines-submissions/

TALOS PRESS
a division of Sky Horse Publishing

GEARED UP WRITING STEAMPUNK

Steampunk not mentioned by name but they do note
Fantasy, Science Fiction and Horror
No word count given
No mention of an agent required either
But they want a Marketing Analysis with submissions,
Don't want to see the entire ms, so check what they do want
https://www.skyhorsepublishing.com/talos-press/submissions/
Reports in 4 to 6 weeks

TARTARUS PRESS
UK Fantasy and Horror publisher
Their website says they are interested in
"literary strange/supernatural fiction"
If you have supernatural elements in your Steampunk
that might be of interest to them
They do calls for submissions, novels 75,000 to 120,000 words
They also do short story collections that add up to the same word count
http://tartaruspress.com/submissions.html?LMCL=t5VGbm

TELL-TALE PUBLISHING
Imprint for Steampunk is Stargazer
(and Déjà vu for reprints)
Very hard to read submissions page
(small narrow font against dark color background)
So, go to this page instead
https://www.tell-talepublishing.com/guidelines.html

TELOS PUBLISHING
A UK publisher with a specific Steampunk line
https://telos.co.uk/steampunk-visions/
no work counts given or mention of agents
however, they are only open for submissions at specific periods
so you'll need to check their website for dates

TITAN PRESS
Most of their releases were licensed from overseas publishers

GEARED UP WRITING STEAMPUNK

BUT they are interested in writers who would like
To work on licensed content they have contracted
Who knows – it could be a way to get your foot in the door
https://titanbooks.com/help/page/submissions/
Steampunk was not specifically mentioned but
they rereleased James Blaylock's Steampunk titles

TOR/FORGE/ORBIT
NIGHTFIRE (horror)
Tom Doherty Associates
Agented and unagented accepted
Website they are not accepting full length novels
Tor is interested in novellas now, 20,000 to 40,000 words
www.tor.com/submissions-guidelines/#Fiction%20Submission%20Guidelines
However, I also found a page for novel submission that
Harkened back to the snail mail/paper submission, too
Find those guidelines at
www.us.macmillan.com/torforge/about/faq/#submit writing

THE TWELFTH PLANET PRESS
An Australian publisher of sci-fi, fantasy and horror
While I didn't find Steampunk titles or a specific interest mentioned,
They might be interested in Steam set in Australia
They've moved their office from one side of the continent
to the other and then back again, latest move December 2019,
So haven't have general submissions opened but should be
up and running again soon, so check them out
http://www.twelfthplanetpress.com/

TYCHE BOOKS
Publishes Steampunk and Slipstream
60,000 to 120,000 words.
Recommends writers push the boundaries!
http://www.tychebooks.com/submissions

GEARED UP WRITING STEAMPUNK

WORLD WEAVER PRESS
Novellas to Novels, so 20,000 to 100,000 words
Steampunk, Dieselpunk and Decopunk
specifically noted as of interest
https://www.worldweaverpress.com/submit-fiction.html

Here's another way to find a publisher (or an agent):
www.manuscriptwishlist.com
Editors and agents post what they are looking for here
You can also check on Twitter **#MSWL**
You cannot post with this hash tag, but you can use it
to find recent posts by the folks who can get you in print

Of course, there is always the Independent Publishing route. Quite a few of the Steampunk books I pulled up at Amazon. Either didn't have a publisher's name noted, or the name given was the authors. Many of these books had a decent place on the sales list, too.

I will note that the ones with the best placement tended to have awesome covers – it helps

AND THAT'S
ALL THERE IS TO IT

...which, of course, makes it sound like a slam dunk, a drop in the bucket, when it's really a lot of hard work, fevered creation, and fast pounding fingers, spilling the story unraveling in your flights of fancy onto the printed page – or computer screen.

You can do it. I have faith in you. In fact, I'd enjoy hearing of your success, that moment when an editor says, "we'd like to offer you a contract on (fill in the title of your book)". It's a truly magical moment.

FEED AN AUTHOR
WRITE AND POST A REVIEW!
Appreciate it!

Beth Daniels has written fiction under several various pseudonyms and for a variety of publishing houses in various genre niches. Besides novel length stories and books about writing, she has scribbled numerous non-fiction writing related articles for e-zines and presided over online workshops with over sixty different fiction or historical research related topics. Having held several *real*-life jobs, including teaching college level composition and communication courses, she now revels in worlds of her own creation, leaning more toward fantasy and mystery.

GEARED UP WRITING STEAMPUNK

Visit
www.4TaleTellers.com

For Steampunk and Dieselpunk fiction
by Nied Darnell

Printed in Great Britain
by Amazon